# A Conscious Endeavor

# A Conscious Endeavor
A Judeo-Christian Reflection
on the Distribution of Wealth

TERENCE WENZL

FOREWORD BY
JOSEPH P. CHINNICI

WIPF & STOCK · Eugene, Oregon

A CONSCIOUS ENDEAVOR
A Judeo-Christian Reflection on the Distribution of Wealth

Copyright © 2014 Terence Wenzl. All rights reserved. Except for brief quotations in critical publications or reviews, no part of this book may be reproduced in any manner without prior written permission from the publisher. Write: Permissions. Wipf and Stock Publishers, 199 W. 8th Ave., Suite 3, Eugene, OR 97401.

Wipf and Stock
An Imprint of Wipf and Stock Publishers
199 W. 8th Ave., Suite 3
Eugene, OR 97401

www.wipfandstock.com

ISBN 13: 978-1-61097-366-3

Manufactured in the U.S.A.                                        12/15/2014

Except where otherwise noted, Scripture quotations are from The Jerusalem Bible, copyright © 1966 by Darton, Longman & Todd, Ltd. and Doubleday, a division of Bantam Doubleday Dell Publishing Group, Inc. Reprinted by permission.

This book is dedicated to my wife Christine my best friend and fan. Thank you, my love.

# Contents

*Foreword by Joseph P. Chinnici* | ix
*Acknowledgments* | xi

Introduction | 1
1  Right Relationships | 7
2  What Is Conversion? | 13
3  How Conversion Happens | 23
4  Reflections on Organized Religion and Biblical Inspiration | 28
5  Old Testament Teaching Regarding Justice and Distribution | 50
6  New Testament Teachings Regarding Justice and Distribution | 68
7  Defining the Task | 89
8  Property Rights | 95
9  Distribution of Wealth and Just Wages | 103
10 Environmentalism | 114
11 Classical Economic Theory | 122
12 Life with Corporations | 133
13 The National Interest | 142
14 Profits | 150
15 Community | 157
Conclusion | 160

*Bibliography* | 165

# Foreword
## The Just Man Justices

WHAT HAPPENS IF YOU take a strong Midwestern heritage, transplant it into the Oregon frontier, nurture it in a large family of brothers and sisters, mix it with high intelligence and iron will, endow it with a capacity for straightforward talking and wonderful storytelling, fill it with a sensitivity for poetry, music, and literature, energize it with a passion for justice and equality, and, above all, grace all of this with a biblical and sacramental faith informed by the vision of St. Francis of Assisi? Any reader exposed to this "conscious endeavor" of life will begin to comprehend the riches of the witness and strength of the author of this book.

I first met Terry Wenzl in the fall of 1963 as we both entered a small college run by the Franciscan friars of the western United States. This was a time of great transitions as the society convulsed with the civil rights movement, the war on poverty, and the struggle against the Vietnam War. At the same time, the Catholic Church recovered a more universal sense of its true identity and its commitment to embrace "the joy and hope, the grief and anguish of the men and women of our time, especially of those who are poor or afflicted in any way . . ." Although our setting at an old mission of Spanish heritage founded in 1798 encouraged long hours of study combined with hard work on a farm, the doors of the mission, the minds and hearts of our professors, and certainly the tenor of our education opened outwards towards the world. Exposed to great books in the classical tradition and accompanied by accomplished classmates, we both aspired at that time to become Catholic priests and Franciscan friars. Terry and I spent the next nine years together. During the time of college, and later as we both migrated to our theology studies in Berkeley in 1968 (!), Terry discovered what was always there: a passion to work for justice for the poor.

FOREWORD

He entered VISTA, spent a year in Florida, and began to construct a vision combining education, social justice, and the Catholic faith. A large man with a searching mind and a soaring soul, he is a continuing inspiration to me and all those who work with him. I have been honored to be his friend for over fifty years.

Eventually our author, who learns through both practice and speculation, worked in the Los Angeles city and county jails. He lived, ate, and suffered with the people of the barrio. He labored with the grape pickers in central California and travelled the back roads of Utah in search of those forgotten. He met the love of his life and raised a family. Terry obtained a contractor's license and for thirty years has been instrumental in creating self-help housing programs in California and Colorado. He has done all of this, as he would be the first to say, with others. To this very day he continues to preach and live the social message of the gospel rooted in Isaiah 61 and Matthew 25:31–46.

*A Conscious Endeavor* bristles with insight and passion. It combines poetic sensitivity with concrete experience and practical wisdom. It is a work not simply to be read but pondered. The author here desires not simply to communicate a wisdom of life but to change hearts. An unusual work, it is the fruit of a uniquely graced person who not only "hears the Word but does it." May the reader enjoy! The "just man justices."

Joseph P. Chinnici, OFM
Franciscan School of Theology
Oceanside, California

# Acknowledgments

THIS BOOK COULD NOT have come to fruition had it not been for the love and support of the following Franciscan Friars: Fr. Alfred Boedecker, OFM, Fr. Louis Vitale, OFM, Fr. Oliver Lynch, OFM, Brother Ed Dunn, OFM, Fr. Pierre Etchelecu, OFM, and Fr. Joseph Chinnici, OFM, one of my dearest friends and a deeply loved brother. All these Friars have left in their wake a deeper understanding of love and justice where little or none existed before they arrived on the scene.

I am also deeply grateful to Christian Amondson, Matthew Wimer, Nathan Rhoads and all the wonderful folks at Wipf and Stock who worked on my manuscript to get it ready for publication.

Last, but not least, I thank Howard Pelham, now deceased, for all he taught me in finding my writing voice. Wherever you are in the Universe, Howard, thank you. You'll always have a special place in my heart.

# Introduction

A FEW YEARS BACK I regularly joined business colleagues for lunch. We dined together every two or three weeks. Because my associates knew I had been a Catholic priest, and had an abiding interest in doing the right thing in their businesses, they often raised ethical questions that dealt with everyday business decisions: How much profit is a reasonable profit? What exactly are my responsibilities to my investors? How can I relate my work life to my home life? . . . etc.

To be sure, responses to these inquiries were as varied and unique as each of us who joined in the discussions. I am not sure we ever solved or completely answered the problems and questions we raised. But the discussion helped us focus on important issues. Grappling with them made each of us more reflective as we went about our daily business lives, and inspired us to search for answers that would apply to our unique or particular circumstances.

While a majority of our population has at one time or other been exposed to Judeo-Christian teachings, these traditions rarely seem to directly address our secular or socio-economic relationships. Rather, there seems to be an unspoken understanding that religious or spiritual values have nothing to add to our daily working lives regarding everyday business decisions. I am not disputing here the conclusions written into the United States Constitution by our founding fathers regarding the separation of church and state. I am speaking of an ethical backdrop that for many could be helpful when discussing formations of partnerships, treatment of the environment, reasonable returns on investment, reasonable profits, and many other socio-economic situations and decisions with which we all must grapple from time to time.

For many, making daily business decisions results in ethical schizophrenia. We separate our thought processes about the way we support ourselves (our economic life and our "work") from other reflective processes (religious or philosophical) about "life" questions (i.e., Why are we here? Where are we going? What happens when we die?).

Let me give you an example. From 1995 to 2000 I lived in Colorado. In 1997 all the Safeway and King Supers grocery chain employees went on strike. The issues in strikes are always complex. A local Catholic nun who administered the social concerns office for the Catholic Diocese of Denver, Colorado, wrote an editorial in one of the local papers explaining why Catholics might want to support the strikers and not cross the picket line. Two days later, the local Catholic bishop publicly took exception to what the nun had said. He essentially said that Catholics should disregard the nun's op-ed piece and follow their conscience in the matter.

Now if the issue had been abortion or some dogma of the Catholic Church, the bishop wouldn't have been so nonchalant. He would have given very specific instructions for people to consider.

With a population of approximately 1.5 million people, the 14,000 Safeway and King Supers strikers represented slightly less than 1 percent of the Denver metropolitan area population—a significant number of people. This group represented a large number of people focusing their attention on some important issues dealing with the rights and duties of both employers and employees. A spiritual leader could have used this opportunity to help nurture a deeper reflection on the underlying values operating in the employer-employee relationship. What was at stake? What issues were the strikers raising that were reasonable? What were the strikers demanding that might have been unreasonable? What were their responsibilities to their employer? What are their responsibilities to the men and women who need to purchase food? I am sure the reader can identify other potential issues to discuss in such a situation that could have taken advantage of the focused attention of the whole Denver metropolitan area on a serious issue and brought them to a deeper level of reflection and growth.

In the end, the bishop's cavalier dismissal of one woman's appropriate reflection caused the serious loss of an opportunity for serious discussion of socio-economic relationships from a Judeo-Christian point of view in a public forum. The Catholic leadership was supporting the alienation of religious reflection from socio-economic realities, and in doing so denied a rich tradition that has much to say on these issues. Ironically, this same bishop was raised to the cardinalate in the Catholic Church and is in Rome in charge of issues regarding the laity.

## INTRODUCTION

Another example: Years ago in Delano, California, I had the opportunity to work with the Franciscan friars in a parish composed mostly of lower-income farm-working families of Mexican-American or Filipino descent living on the west side of town. Most of these men and women were members of the United Farm Workers Union, a union organized to obtain economic justice for farm workers.

There was another Catholic parish in Delano, on the east side of town. The Catholic growers attended this parish. Ironically, one parish became known as the Growers' Parish and the other became known as the Workers Union Parish. Again, what the Church was showing by this unconscious separation of rich and poor into two different parishes was that the same gospel would not be, or could not be, lived out the same way in both settings. This is a classic example of the schizophrenia I refer to.

My purpose in writing this book is to encourage a reflective process that can be called transcendental in the American tradition of the transcendentalists: Emerson, Whitman, Thoreau, and others. In addition I would like to examine our economic life from the standpoint of the Judeo-Christian tradition. My purpose in doing this is not to proselytize. Nor is my purpose to provide answers. What I hope to do is ask the right questions. Can a social teaching be derived from the Scriptures of the Judeo-Christian tradition? What is this tradition, if there is one? What is the mindset the Scriptures define and encourage regarding the use of the world's goods, profits, and other "worldly" or "secular" issues regarding our relationship to the world, its good, and the distribution of wealth?

As a matter of fact, there is a point of view expressed in these traditions that talks about social relationships, how we consume, and our use of the earth's goods. While this point of view might not express exactly how much per hour an employer should pay their employees, it is not without direction in these matters.

Our journey will necessitate some reflection on the Old Testament and the New Testament, and the very nature of revelation itself. The task will be to make relevant to the present day certain scriptural values discussed in a different time and culture. We will need to discuss basic scriptural concepts and what we mean by "revelation." We will find we must relate what we call biblical revelation to other revelations we experience and see how the concept of revelation needs to be understood within a broader context in order to grasp the beauty and intent of its uniqueness.

## A Conscious Endeavor

What we stand to gain are certain truths that can serve to guide us at the present time. When truth is spoken, most men and women of truth recognize it. Emerson reflects in his "Essay on Nature" on the sun-like quality of truth and writes that there is a universality to truth that shines forth and speaks to all people.[1] All people recognize truth. This does not mean we are always ready to hear and accept truth when it is revealed to us. Even though we recognize what is truth, we often turn away because we are not ready to deal with the inner changes that truth will demand from us.

Truth has greater value than the sectarian dogmas of a particular religious group, and was certainly meant to have a wider appeal and importance than that. The values that derive from the Scriptures are meant to have a universal message and appeal. Walt Whitman, an American poet, expresses best this idea in his poem "The Base of All Metaphysics":

> And now, Gentlemen,
> A word I give to remain in your memories and minds,
> As base and finale too for all metaphysics.
>
> (So to the students the old professor,
> At the close of his crowded course.)
>
> Having studied the new and antique, the Greek and Germanic systems,
> Kant having studied and stated, Fichte and Schelling, and Hegel,
> Stated the lore of Plato, and Socrates greater than Plato,
> And greater than Socrates sought and stated, Christ divine having studied long,
> I see reminiscent today those Greek and Germanic systems,
> See the philosophies all, Christian churches and tenets see,
> Yet underneath Socrates clearly see, and underneath Christ the divine I see,
> The dear love of man for his comrade, the attraction of Friend to friend,
> Of the well-married husband and wife, of children and parents,
> Of City for City, and Land for Land.[2]

The journey I would like you to travel with me reflects the point of view of a man who, first as a friar and later as a businessman, has spent his life working with lower-income people and for the betterment of their lives

---

1. Emerson, "Essay on Nature," in *Selected Writings*, 12.
2. Whitman, "The Base of All Metaphysics," in *Leaves of Grass*, 101–2.

## Introduction

together with others. It represents a point of view based on that experience. It will not be one that can give all the answers. However, the direction and tone of the discussion of social relationships through reflection on transcendental ideas and scriptural values would best be described as reflections about justice.

If we can raise the right questions, we can trust that men and women of good will, reflective people interested in their own inner change, will find the answers to these questions in a manner that addresses directly their particular lives and relationships.

My own education was in the liberal arts. I studied literature, philosophy, history, and art. Later on, as a Franciscan friar, I studied theology. I have been very grateful for the education I received. It has helped me reflect deeply and richly on the religious and humanist traditions developed through Western culture. This education has helped me reflect deeply, and develop a critical way of thinking about the culture in which I live. This education has convinced me that we would all be better served if men and women who go to college were able to spend some time in the humanities before specializing in some field of knowledge that is more geared towards employment than reflection. In his essay "The Idea of a University," Cardinal John Henry Newman reflects on what education is really about. In short, he reflects on how the whole idea of a university is to help us find our place in the universe as an individual and as a member of the community of humankind. An education should give us a "universal" or, one might even say, "cosmic" reflection regarding where we come from and where we are going—why we are here. I've noticed a difference in education today. Too often higher education seems related to job training than to reflections on our place in the universe and an introduction to methods of critical thinking.

Most students pick a college major that is job related. There are many people today who might graduate from college having never been exposed to the ideas of Socrates, Aristotle, Augustine, Ockham, Thomas Aquinas, Shakespeare, Milton, Bacon, Locke, Hume, Thoreau, Wordsworth, Emerson, Whitman, Matthew Arnold, Jefferson, Samuel Adams—to mention a few.

This saddens me. I think of a liberal education as akin to the prayer beads of Buddhist monks. Each bead represents a "mantra" or "holy thought" that the monk will repeat over and over again. The monks believe that by repeating holy words one will get lost in holy thoughts.

## A Conscious Endeavor

If one is often exposed to transcendent ideas, one is encouraged to forge one's life after those ideas. If we are not exposed to them, we might not live so elevated a life. Emerson writes in his essay "The Poet":

> It takes a good deal of time to eat or to sleep, or to earn a hundred dollars, and a very little time to entertain a hope and an insight which becomes the light of our life.[3]

I believe it is the lack of this type of reflection and exposure to our loftier possibilities that encouraged Thoreau to write, "The mass of men lead lives of quiet desperation."

I hope this discussion will not only raise some of the right questions, but will raise the level of the discussion as well. Hopefully the bibliography might become a jumping-off point for many who might not otherwise have wanted to investigate the people Whitman mentions in his poem above.

---

3. Emerson, "The Poet," in *Selected Writings*, 301.

# 1
# Right Relationships

WHEN I WAS TWENTY-FOUR years old, I worked in the South as a Vista Volunteer for a year and a half. While in the South I decided to go to Mardi Gras in New Orleans. At the time I had long hair and a beard. The year was 1968. I had stopped in a small Southern town to get some gas for my old Volkswagen. While I was filling my gas tank, I was accosted by a man of the Baptist persuasion who had been recently redeemed. He literally backed me into a corner and asked, "Have y'all been saved?" I said, "What do you mean, 'Have I been saved?'" He replied, "Have y'all been saved? Y'all had a day and an hour and a minute when you was saved? If you cain't tell me the day, the hour, and the minute when you was saved, then y'all ain't been saved."

I think he figured there would be very few times in his life when he would have the chance to "save" a hippy. I thought about what he said and responded, "Look, Mister, I don't remember much about being born, but I sure was born. I don't think memory has much to do with whether or not a person is saved."

Later on, when I studied theology in the Catholic Church I wondered why people used the term "saved" as if it were something that could happen in a moment. It seemed to me a term that had lost its meaning.

One day I was reading an author whose name I cannot now remember. He explained how the word "salvation" came from Roman medical terminology, derived from the Latin word *salvus*. When a person gets cut, for example, the skin is separated. As part of curing the wound, one might apply what we call a "salve," and the skin broken and torn apart would be brought back together. It becomes *salvus*, that is, healed.

The author explained how early Christians took this medical term and applied it to relationships. He then began to explain how in Christian belief there is a rift in the relationship between God and humans, something that requires "healing" of the relationship. What Jesus shows people is a way to become *salvus*, or healed, in our relationships to God, ourselves, others, and nature.

If we read the New Testament carefully, we would say that Jesus was completely focused on reconciliation, forgiveness, and healing. He wanted people to take stock of and come to terms with their relationship to God and others.

Emerson in his "Essay on Nature" says, "We are as much strangers in nature as we are aliens from God."[1] The Transcendentalists believed God revealed the divine presence in nature. For them, to the extent that we alienate ourselves from nature, we alienate ourselves from God. There is a sense of alienation and separateness we all experience deep within ourselves. This feeling is like a deep ache, which often indicates how out of touch we are with our own soul, let alone from others. For example, many who live in large cities feel no sense of community. Many in this environment feel cut off from most of their fellow human beings. One can look at New York City or Los Angeles and see more a large group of individuals than a vibrant human community.

Some religions call this sense of separation and aloneness "original sin"; some "fate"; some "caste." There is something at the heart of our relationships to ourselves and others that is often out of whack.

Emerson also suggests there are experiences we have with nature that make us feel deeply at peace and closer to God. In the movie *Jeremiah Johnson*, an otherwise rather disreputable character named Dale Q at one point exclaims as he rides off into the mountains, "There are no finer church spires than these here Rocky Mountains, and no better place created by the Almighty."

Our life's task is to bring ourselves from fractured and broken relationships back into Right Relationships. The process by which we do this is what I will call inner change or conversion. Conversion does not happen all at once, like the gentleman in the gas station believed. For some people, being set on the road to conversion might be initiated by a dramatic event, but that is just the beginning. Inner change takes a long, long time. It takes a lifetime. Your inner changes might be initiated by profound experiences

---

1. Emerson, "Essay on Nature," in *Selected Writings*, 33.

in nature, or in human relationships. Your discovery of the value of life, for instance, might be initiated by the birth of your own son or daughter. Your realization of the value of human relationships might be initiated by the death of someone for whom you cared deeply. Your inner change might be brought about in struggles for social justice and experiences of solidarity with those who are disenfranchised. Experiences that lead to the awakening in our souls of the call to inner change are not necessarily peaceful or positive. The experience that awakens us to who we are and why we are here might be very painful and negative in our initial understanding.

For my oldest brother, Don, it was such. If there was ever a person who reminded me of Job, it was he. Don was struck with polio at age nineteen, and would live out the rest of his life in a wheelchair. He became the first paraplegic to graduate from the University of Oregon. This was before the time of such things as curb cuts, wheelchair ramps, and disabled parking spaces. Later in life he became blind. While blind he earned a doctoral degree in educational counseling.

While Job had his worldly suffering end and his wealth returned, my brother did not. Still, he did not give up on life. One time he said to me, "Terry, everyone has handicaps. I am lucky to know what many of mine are." He also related to me that although there were numerous times he had contemplated suicide, he never would take his own life. And to watch his joyful demeanor, you would never think suicide could have crossed his mind.

Living in a wheelchair and being blind slowed Don down. He became a great listener and effective counselor. He had time to listen. He was not in a hurry to be about some other business. I was repeatedly amazed at how many lives he touched. People would tell me things like, "When I was going through a tough time in my life, he really helped me out," or, "He always had time to listen to my problems," or, "He never complained about his burdens, and this seemed to make it easier for me to carry mine."

Don would never tell you what a great thing it was for him to have his ability to walk taken away. Nor would he tell you what a wonderful thing it was to be blind. What Don would tell you is that you have to identify your limitations, accept them, and move on.

Don's situation and the concept of conversion remind me of an idea put forward by the composer Igor Stravinsky. Stravinsky reflected that if you offered him a piano with an infinite number of keys, he would compose nothing. But if you limited him to eighty-eight notes, then he could create wonderful musical compositions. Stravinsky concluded that in order to be creative one has to work through very clear limitations. Each of us must learn and accept our limits. In Don's case, he had to accept and work through his inability to walk and see physically to discover his creative genius as a counselor in seeing deeply into the lives of others and helping them to move or walk forward in their own lives. Often times knowing what our limitations are is relatively easy. Accepting and working through them is far and away where our difficulties lie. It is one thing to have my ability to walk or see taken away from me and to know in my mind those abilities are not coming back. It is quite another to accept in my heart and soul this totally absurd situation without bitterness, and to continue my life in a positive and loving manner, eventually creating genius and redemption where others might have seen only suffering and loss. Yet this is the miracle we accomplish in our life of conversion. Just as Don had to deal with some very difficult limitations, each of us has difficult situations that can lead to conversion, positive inner change, and growth if we rise to the challenge.

Conversion, as I said, does not always come from a positive experience. But conversion will shape what we do with present experiences and how we let it mold our future. This is the qualitative difference I am trying to describe.

Many times it is only in retrospect we can look at a certain experience or number of experiences and understand that they were moments of conversion. These may become events we will recall as experiences of the Divine, or times of intense insight, or inner peace, which brought about in us changes that led to positive growth and deepening.

In Rio Grande, Texas, there is a group of Mexican-American citizens who for five generations has followed the crop harvest from Texas up through New Mexico, Colorado, Utah, and Oregon. They end up in Yakima Valley, Washington, harvesting apples. They are paid less than an appropriate wage. However, they live simply and send their money home to their American families in Rio Grande.

One day my friend Ed Dunne was talking with one of these men. "Jose," Ed said to him, "every year you work your way from Texas to the Yakima Valley. You live in housing that's quite a few notches below substandard. You are paid meager wages. You're in dangerous working conditions. You're afforded no medical services. You work fourteen-hour days. You know it'll always be the same. Why do you do it?" Jose looked at Ed and responded, "Ed, if we do not harvest the crops, the people will have nothing to eat."

## Right Relationships

Here was a man who understood the dignity of work and its importance even though the people who paid him to harvest their crops did not. Listening to this young Mexican-American husband, father, and field worker reflect on the importance of what he does hit Ed right between the eyes. It was a powerful moment, a moment of conversion. Ed explained to me how moments such as these continually keep him dedicated to working toward a world in which there are more just human relationships. We all have such experiences that offer us conversion.

In California, at the height of the Grape Strike led by the United Farm Workers Union, I had the occasion to have dinner with some friends who were quite well off financially. It was a Sunday dinner. The mother happened to be a supporter of the union strike. Her son-in-law was on the other side of the issue. At one point in the discussion he asked almost cynically, "Do you actually think your not eating table grapes is going to change the situation for farm workers?"

She thought a moment, and said, "I really cannot say for certain if my not eating table grapes is going to change the situation for farm workers. But I'll tell you this, not eating table grapes and the reasons why I don't has changed me."

Whether this process of conversion, of inner change, begins dramatically or not, for most of us it is a quiet change that takes a very long time, a little bit at a time. A young Buddhist monk was being taught meditation by his teacher. When the teacher thought he was finished teaching a certain method of meditation, he said to his student, "Do this every day for one hour, and in twenty years you might begin to notice a difference."[2] The change in ourselves is like this.

Conversion is not the privilege of only those who claim to be men and women of faith, who believe in God, who belong to an organized religion. It may happen there, and maybe one has the right to expect it to happen there more often. But all of us are offered many opportunities and experiences that can lead to inner change. It is this inner change, conversion, that will bring us back into Right Relationships with ourselves, with others, nature, and with God.

After many years of reading the Old Testament and New Testament I have become convinced that their central theme is Right Relationships. Forming Right Relationships is the result of inner conversion and an examined life. For only through changing ourselves can we make things right. As

---

2. Rinpoche, *Tibetan Book of Living and Dying*, 60–79.

the years have passed I've realized the most substantial change that we can effect is the change within ourselves.

In our own time, those who offer themselves as representing the essence of mainstream religion seem to be lost in the gas station world of my Baptist friend who wanted to "save" me. I am sure that with the best of intentions, he did not have the slightest idea what that meant. It is *not* understanding conversion that has lead major religions and religious denominations to beat around the bush. They place at the center of religion those things that have the least importance or stand in direct opposition to scriptural teaching.

For instance, in the Catholicism in which I was raised, the sacraments were viewed as central, as the defining reality of what it means to be a Catholic. Particular emphasis was placed on Mass. Inner conversion was alluded to from time to time, but it never quite made it to the core.

For other groups it might be some vague notion of "accepting Jesus as your personal savior" or "being saved." This has lead to very destructive behaviors. Being off center allowed the Catholic Church to question whether or not American natives had souls, the Inquisition in Spain, the Crusades, and other horrors committed in the name of religion. It allowed Southern Baptists to justify slavery. It allowed Puritans in Salem to burn "witches." It allowed Lutherans in Germany to obey the Third Reich and not question it as a legitimate authority.

But if we emphasize Right Relationships, we will keep the center where it ought to be. As we continue this reflection we will need to examine a bit more closely this concept of conversion and how it happens. This will prepare us for some discussion of Old and New Testament social values and reflections on the use of the world's goods. From there we will be able to look at classical economic theories and through comparison raise some legitimate questions and issues for our consideration.

# 2
# What Is Conversion?

When I try to explain conversion, I find it is best to examine the origin of the word. Conversion does not mean to become a member of an organized religion, though popular usage certainly tends in that direction. The word *conversion* is derived from the Latin verb *convertire*, which means "to turn around." When applied to inner or spiritual growth, it refers to that change inside a person which begins with the realization that his/her life needs to take a substantially different direction.

This different direction is essentially a spiritual direction. For some people it might be the first time in their lives they have realized their own hunger for God. For most, if not all of us, this "waking up" or coming to an awareness of the reality of God and/or a spiritual life is very much integrated with finding our true self. The great Jewish mystic Martin Buber claimed that all of us have access to God, but each of has a different access. Our great opportunity to find God lies precisely in our unlikeness to each other. God's all-inclusiveness manifests itself in the infinite multiplicity of the ways that lead to him, each of which is open only to one person.

Of course, this is why self-knowledge is so important. In order to find God, we must be brutally honest with ourselves. In short, we must become ourselves. You have heard the expression "be yourself," and that is exactly what we must do. We are not called to be somebody else or to lead someone else's life or spirituality. We are called to forge a spirituality, a spirit life, that is unique to us in the sense that our own spiritual search helps us find God in a way that is real for us and leads us to a deeper life in which we live out our relationships in our uniquely "God-filled" way. The Rabbi Zusya, a well respected Hassidic Rabbi, said, "In the world to come, I shall not be asked: 'Why were you not Moses?' I shall be asked: 'Why were you not Zusya?'"

While it might take a very long time to discover what that new direction is, once a person has the initial realization that a new direction is in order, then conversion has begun.

St. Francis of Assisi, a thirteenth-century man whose personal life and conversion are world famous, began this process out of some dramatic life experiences.

During the time of Francis Bernadone, the Middle Ages were in decline, the Renaissance in Italy was just around the corner, and a merchant class had emerged. Francis's father, Pietro, was a member of this new merchant class. The family would have been considered upper middle class by today's standards.

Most countries like Germany, France, Italy, and Spain did not have truly national identities. Instead, city-states existed within these regions. These city-states were often at war. Assisi would war with Perugia, a neighboring city-state. During one of these conflicts, Francis was captured and was imprisoned for a year. Upon his return his friends and neighbors noticed how this normally jubilant, boisterous, always-ready-for-a-party young man had now become more serious and reflective.

Francis recounts a particularly powerful experience between himself and a man with leprosy. It happened soon after his return from war. Leprosy was then greatly feared as it was thought to be highly contagious (you might think of it as we think of AIDS today). He describes riding through the country one day and meeting one of the most contagious-looking lepers he had ever seen, begging alms in the name of God at the side of the road.

The sight and smell of this man were so overwhelming and disgusting that both Francis and his horse raced off in panic and fear. He was finally able to rein in his horse and think. He concluded, "If this had been someone who had come into your father's cloth shop and asked for something in the name of one of your father's wealthy friends, you would have given it to him. This man asked for something in the name of God, and you denied it." Francis rode back, got off his horse, and gave the leper alms, then embraced him. Later in his life, Francis would reflect:

> When I was in sin, the sight of lepers nauseated me beyond measure; but when God himself led me into their company, at first I had pity on them. Then, as I became acquainted with them, what

had previously nauseated me became a source of spiritual and physical consolation for me.[1]

Francis indicates both in his becoming more reflective as a prisoner of war and his actions with the leper that his views on life and its meaning were changing. What is particularly important about the encounter with the leper was that Francis's nausea had more to do with his own lack of understanding that this was a human being with leprosy, not a leper. In other words, having a Right Relationship with himself and the man with leprosy became the reality. Once he came to this realization, he was able to turn his horse around, go back, and have an exchange of human kindness with a fellow human being.

Francis realized that many of his relationships became Right Relationships when they included compassion for another human being. Certainly Francis gave alms to a person with leprosy, but this man gave Francis a far greater gift: the gift of human friendship. Before this experience friendship with "lepers" was not only alien to his perception, but an impossibility. Before this experience, Francis viewed people with leprosy as less than human, and outside his sphere of relating. In the future he would see lepers as men and women with the same dignity he possessed. Further relationships, even friendships, with a whole new group of human beings was made possible. Francis's experience is this regard is certainly something all of us experience in every period of history. Each of us has probably been guilty of excluding from our sphere of relating whole groups of people just because of who they are. Most often these exclusions are based on race, economic status, and religion.

In his novel *Sacred Clowns*, Tony Hillerman has Navajo sheriff's deputy Jim Chee describe an aspect of Navajo spiritual approaches to a young Navajo friend named Janet. Janet, like Jim Chee, had left the reservation to go to college. She received a law degree. Both returned to the reservation. Jim Chee, besides being a reservation sheriff's deputy, is from a clan that has provided holy men to his tribe. He is therefore consciously aspiring to become a holy man as he studies the Beauty Way of his people. He is seeking conversion.

Most recently a Native American has been found dead in a parking lot, apparently run over by a car. He and Janet are discussing what ought to be done with the person who did this when he or she is apprehended.

---

1. Francis of Assisi, "Testament of Francis," in *St. Francis of Assisi*, 67.

## A Conscious Endeavor

Deputy Chee contrasts American legal justice with the Navajo idea of justice on which he was raised:

> We'll say the cop is religious. He honors his people's traditional ways. He has been taught another notion of justice. He was a big boy before he heard about . . . "an eye for an eye, a tooth for a tooth." Instead of that he was hearing . . . If you damage somebody, you sit down and make it good. That way you restore *hosho*. You've got harmony again between two families . . . if somebody harms you out of meanness . . . then he's the one who's out of *hosho*. You aren't taught he should be punished. He should be cured, gotten back in balance with what's around him, made beautiful again. . . . It is because of how you understand the Beauty Way. . . . I'll use an example: Terrible drought. Crops dead. Sheep dying. Spring dried out. No water. The Hopi, or the Christian, maybe the Moslem, they pray for rain. The Navajo has the proper ceremony done to restore himself to harmony with the drought.[2]

Richard Niebuhr has said: "Lord grant me the serenity to accept the things I cannot change, the courage to change the things that I can; and the wisdom to know the difference."

This whole process of conversion begins with self-examination. It does not begin with examining and judging the life of someone else as wanting or needing improvement. Nor am I talking here about some kind of unhealthy self-centered psychological analysis of ourselves. It is not a process that begins with us listening to the same old record over and over again, reveling in self-pity, romantic pessimism, or some exaggerated sense of self-worth. I am not talking about getting in touch with your inner child, or I'm OK and you're OK, or men are from Mars, etc.

The process begins with a realization steeped in humility and hope at the same time. The late Thomas Merton, a Trappist monk, had many things to say about the process of conversion. Merton says the saints are not what they are not because they are admired and loved by everybody else. People whom we consider holy or saints are what they are because *they* admire and love everybody else. The saint has realized that he/she is as human and sinful as everyone else, and that we all stand in need of the love and mercy of God.[3]

We often waste much of our lives looking for some guru so that we can have his/her experience or live out his/her spirituality. We can wear

---

2. Hillerman, *Sacred Clowns*, 315–16.
3. Merton, *New Seeds of Contemplation*, 57.

## What Is Conversion?

ourselves out in this. Socrates spent his life searching for a truly wise man who could teach him. However, he always found something lacking in those who presented themselves as teachers. For this reason he began asking questions, critically looking at people's assumptions about life and reality. Gautama Siddhartha came to a point of understanding that no one could be his teacher, but that he must find his own path to enlightenment. Essentially, the person who is searching for truth, or God, or inner conversion will take whatever there is in the world that helps him to find God and will leave the rest aside.[4]

Conversion then begins with a realization of who we are. It is not just a rational or emotional experience. Conversion is experience of Being, or of what it means *to be*.

Let me give you a couple of examples. It is a wonderfully sunny day in early summer. It is Saturday and you have just gone for a leisurely walk through the woods with a good friend. You decide to stop and rest for a while. You are lying on the ground and looking up at the sky into the dappled sunlight shining through a tree. You can feel the warmth of the sun on your skin as well as the gentleness of a cool breeze off the hillside. Neither you nor your friend is talking. You're aware of how good it is to be here. You are even aware of your enjoyment. You are totally relaxed. You are enjoying being.

Or again, you're in a birthing room with your wife. Your child has just come out of the womb and has been placed in your wife's arms. While for the last three hours there has been a lot of pain, shouting, heavy breathing, bearing down, and instructions from the doctor and nurses, you are now aware only of your wife, your baby, and you. Even though there are fifteen people in the room chattering away, you hear nothing at all except your baby, you wife's sobs of joy, and your breathing. Hers are joyous, hot tears. At the same time you are engulfed by a great love for your wife and child, and a gratefulness for this great gift of your child, of life itself. This all hits you at the same time. You aren't "thinking," you are in a new state of being, we'll call it "father-being." You have experienced with great force what it means *to be* a father.

When we have such experiences we get a clear understanding of who we are and what it means *to be*. This type of experience transcends the physical, rational, and emotional even though it might include one or all of them.

4. Ibid., 98–99.

## A Conscious Endeavor

The experience of what and who we are as *beings* is at the very heart of conversion. As we begin to lead a more contemplative (reflective) life, we begin to experience the implications of who we are as *Beings* (remember the Buddhist monk and his meditation student?).

When we have these experiences of actually *being* we are stuck by how much more real or worthwhile they are than most of our waking hours. In his book *The Tibetan Book of Living and Dying*, Sogyal Rimpoche discusses in a rather comical way all the things that we must do that we consider our responsibilities: get up in the morning, open the window, make the bed, take a shower, brush your teeth, feed the dog . . . and the list goes on. At the same time he discusses how these responsibilities become excuses for not doing the "important" things in our lives. He says that perhaps we should start calling these things our irresponsibilities instead.[5]

As if this were not enough, how about all the following "stuff": all the positive and negative aspects of the family in which we were raised, all our social relationships, all our business relationships, the political backdrop in which we must operate, our cultural upbringing, our religious upbringing, our emotional life, scars and all, our intellectual ideas . . . and the list goes on. We will need to look at everything from our past, sort it out and decide what to keep and what to discard as we sift through the medium of our lives. As I said before, conversion is real work. It doesn't happen all at once like my Baptist friend in the gas station thought it did.

Conversion begins with humility and hope. The humility begins with realizing we are at the same time less and more than we want to be, that we are pilgrims and wanderers on this earth, that we will die.

The hope is that we can transcend within ourselves those things that have kept us from our own humanity—our angers, our fears, our "stuff" that keeps telling us what we can't do. Our hope is that we can make a difference within ourselves.

In the Introduction to his book *Reveille for Radicals*, Saul Alinski responds in this way when he is asked what he has learned through his years of community organizing:

> I have changed in that I have learned to freeze my hot anger into cool anger, and to make my intuitive irreverence conscious, to challenge not only the opposition but myself, to realize and accept the prime importance of the Socratic adage about the unexamined life. Through action, reflection, study, testing, and synthesis

---

5. Rinpoche, *Tibetan Book of Living and Dying*, 19.

## What Is Conversion?

> I have learned to distill experience from living.... I have learned to search for laws of change, to discover for myself such simple truths that the real action is in the reaction.... In short, cool anger and conscious understanding based on experience have made my actions far more calculated, deliberate, directive, and effective.... I have learned not to confuse power patterns with the personalities of the individuals involved; in other words, to hate conditions, not individuals. Thus I have learned to become in many ways the master rather than the servant of my tactics, and to develop far more effective tactics—economic, political, and social—than the simple, hot, angry, personalized denunciation.... I have also learned to avoid succumbing to a rationale which would permit me the escape of becoming a rhetorical radical and not a radical realist.[6]

Thomas Merton talks in a similar way when discussing the development of nuclear capability in the United States and the whole concept of being a person who is trying to bring peace to a world so intent on building up weapons of mass destruction. He says the key is not loving what we think is peace, but loving others and God above all. If we want a peaceful world, we will realize this is related to achieving inner peace within ourselves. Instead of hating other people whom we think are warmongers, we will need to hate those disorders in our own souls that are the causes of war. If we are to love justice and peace, then we must hate injustice, tyranny, and greed. But we should hate them in ourselves and not in another.[7]

As this conversion process matures, our inner change will lead us to a deeper, fuller humanity. The point of conversion is not to become some spiritualized being who is not related to his/her environment. The opposite is true. As I change inside, the way I relate to every person will be different. Negative things like greed, selfishness, insensitivity to others, etc. will fall by the wayside and will be replaced with a better humanity.

As we spend more time in reflection and quiet, our external actions will begin to flow from a place deep inside of us, our true "being," or true "self." The conversion process is something like this: Suppose that we compare God to sunlight and our soul to a windowpane. All forms of selfishness, hate, evil, prejudices, aversions, and cravings are, when we cling to them, like dirt on the windowpane. The thicker the dirt, the more opaque the window, and the less sun can shine through. When there is no dirt,

---

6. Alinski, *Rules for Radicals*, ix.
7. Merton, *New Seeds of Contemplation*, 122.

the window is by its nature perfectly transparent, and the light can pass through without hindrance.[8]

You will remember earlier we discussed how conversion is a day-by-day process that takes years, even though for some (by no means all) people a particularly powerful experience may initiate them to the process of conversion, as happened to Francis with the man with leprosy. However, when one undergoes a spiritual transformation, he or she is truly reborn. The shape of the personality may be the same and there still may be plenty of weeds we need to pull from our personal gardens. But the old inner self is gone. Integrating the new self we have discovered into all our relationships is the greatest and most difficult task we will have in conversion and spiritual growth.[9]

Mohammed Ali, for me, is an excellent example of this. From the time of his conversion to Islam, there were many things about the shape of his personality that were the same. But through the years one could see a profound deepening of his spirit. At the same time, from the beginning of his discovery of Islam, it was clear to him and to many others that he was on a new path. One of the discoveries in this conversion process—of the Beauty Way as the Navajo would call it—is that as we integrate this new self into our relationships they become Right Relationships.

There are reasons to discuss the process of conversion before entering into a discussion of social values and teachings of the Judeo-Christian tradition as expressed in the Old Testament and the New Testament. The main reason is because it is central to any understanding of social relationships in Scripture.

The Judeo-Christian view of social change is inextricably linked to the conversion of individual minds and hearts. Social change, even positive social change, that is not accompanied by conversion falls short of the scriptural ideal.

Let me give an example. Before the passing of certain civil rights laws in the 1960s in the United States, there existed certain communities, and even whole states, in which racist individuals were able to control communities in such a way that blacks and certain other non-whites could not attend certain schools, live in specified neighborhoods, even drink from certain water fountains. With the passing of civil rights legislation, the federal government was able to enforce the laws to change racist laws, customs,

---

8. Mitchell, *Gospel According to Jesus*, 13–14.
9. Ibid., 51.

## What Is Conversion?

and behavior. As civil rights laws were enforced, certain changes began to occur. These changes were certainly good for the whole country, not just for the minorities who seemed to be the most direct beneficiaries of these laws.

The laws changed the external behavior of racism, but it could not change racists' hearts. In the conversion model, the racist individuals would have come to a spiritual understanding that all men and women have the dignity of being sons and daughters of God, and would therefore have started integrating this belief into all their relationships with all human beings. Treating all with the dignity and respect that they have as a son or daughter of God would become a natural outflow of their true self.

I am not saying that legal correction of bad behavior is to be avoided. Some things are so intolerable that we cannot wait for people to change from the inside. The negative behavior must be stopped. I am only saying that conversion is a more profoundly human and radical response to something that needs changing. For in conversion, people radically change. In his second series of essays of "New England's Reformers," Emerson writes:

> The criticism and attack on institutions, which we have witnessed, has made one thing plain, that society gains nothing whilst a man, not himself renovated, attempts to renovate things around him.[10]

I mentioned above that conversion is a radical response to something that needs changing. I would like to examine the word *radical*. The word comes from the Latin *radix*, which translates as "root" (i.e.; root of a tree or plant, etc.). A radical is a person who gets to the root of things. Popular meaning associates the term with a particular left-wing point of view. But more truly, a radical is a person who gets to the very root of things. No true radical will fit anyone's political agenda, whether liberal or conservative. The true radical will have a more profound reflection to offer on a particular topic, because the observation of the radical man or woman will be about Right Relationships. In his book *Reveille for Radicals* Saul Alinsky defines the radical:

> Whenever America's hearts are breaking, there American radicals were and are.... The hope and future of America lies with its radicals.... What is the American radical? The radical is that unique person who actually believes what he says. He is that person to whom the common good is the greatest personal value. He is that person who genuinely and completely believes in mankind. The radical is so completely identified with mankind that he personally

---

10. In Emerson, *Selected Writings*, 407

shares the pain, the injustices and the suffering of all his fellow men.... What does the radical want? He wants a world in which the worth of the individual is recognized. He wants the creation of a kind of society where all of man's potentialities can be realized; a world where man could live in dignity, security, happiness, and peace—a world based on a morality of mankind.[11]

Conversion is getting to the root of things within ourselves and then integrating that into all our relationships so that they become Right Relationships. It is a radical occurrence. We are all meant to be radicals. As Thomas Paine wrote:

> Let them call me a rebel and welcome, I feel no concern from it, but I should suffer the misery of devils, were I to make a whore of my soul...[12]

---

11. Alinsky, *Reveille for Radicals*, 14–15.
12. Paine, *The American Crisis*, Crisis No. 1.

# 3

# How Conversion Happens

THE PROPHET EZEKIEL WROTE:

> The Lord God says this: I will gather you together from among the peoples, I will bring you all back from the countries where you have been scattered. . . . I will give them a new heart, and I will put a new spirit in them; and I will remove the heart of stone from their bodies and give them a heart of flesh instead, so that they will keep my laws and respect my observances and put them into practice. (Ezek 11:17–21)[1]

I am particularly interested in the phrase that Ezekiel so poetically writes, "I will remove the heart of stone from their bodies and give them a heart of flesh instead." As Stephen Mitchell stated earlier, once we have received our heart of flesh, integrating this new outlook—"faith" or whatever else you want to call it—into our lives is the most difficult aspect of conversion.

We hear a lot of discussion in religious circles in both West and East of overcoming the self or the ego. This is the heart of inner change. What do we mean by this?

In the First Book of Samuel, God sends Samuel to Bethlehem to pick the leader of Israel. Samuel thinks that Eliab is the person to choose because he has a regal bearing, but God tells him:

> Take no notice of his appearance or his height for I have rejected him; God does not see as man sees; for man looks at the outward appearance, but God looks into the heart. (1 Sam 16:7)

---

1. Jerusalem Bible. All scriptural passages used in this discussion will be quoted from this edition.

## A Conscious Endeavor

In the New Testament, it is written that "God does not have respect for persons" (Rom 2:11). What is being said here is important. If we look to where the word *person* comes from we will get a sharper understanding.

We are all familiar with the happy and sad "masks" that represent the comedy and tragedy of drama. We also know these masks are related to classical Greek theater from the times of Sophocles and Xenephon, dating as early as 600 BC.

In ancient Greek theater, actors and actresses did not use makeup as they do in our time. Neither did they have the sound systems with boom microphones as we have today.

For this reason, the Greeks devised masks that represented the characters being portrayed. They had long sticks that were held by the hand of the actor or actress to keep them front of his/her face.

They not only had the likeness of the face of a character in the play (Antigone, Achilles, etc.), but they were also pieces of technical equipment for projecting the actor or actress's voice.

Each mask had a small megaphone (remember the old megaphones that cheer leaders used at football games?) built into it, so that when the actor or actress spoke through it, his/her voice would be projected out to the audience.

In ancient Greek theater, one actor or actress might play two or three parts. To switch roles he/she merely changed masks, and his/her voice was projected through a different mask.

Such a mask was called a *persona*, which is combined from *per-*, meaning "through," and *sona*, which means "sound." *Persona*, then, meant "that through which the sound comes." At the same time, a *persona* was something that an actor or actress placed in front of his/her face in order to appear as someone who in reality he/she was not, i.e., a character(s) in the play.

When we relate this knowledge back to the scriptural passages referred to above, it becomes very clear the writers of Scripture were saying God is not a respecter of *personas*. They meant God does not have any respect for the parts we act out that are not really us. God has no respect for that part of us which tries to represent ourselves as something we are not. God is a God of the heart.

In the Sermon on the Mount, when Jesus is instructing about prayer, he says:

## How Conversion Happens

> And when you pray, do not imitate the hypocrites: they love to say their prayers standing up in the synagogues and at the street corners for people to see them. I tell you solemnly, they have had their reward. But when you pray, go to your private room and, when you have shut your door, pray to your Father who is in that secret place, and your Father who sees all that is done in secret will reward you. (Matt 6:5–6)

What is the secret place? It is the place inside our heart where there are no *personas*. This excerpt from Matthew illustrates very well the difference between the prayerful *persona*, which the hypocrites like to project, and the individual who seriously wishes to pray from the heart.

Jesus is saying that if you truly want to be a prayerful (reflective) human, you have to go away from the hubbub of the world's *personas*. You have to shut the door on it, and enter into that secret place inside your heart where there is only absolute honest conversation between yourself, as you really are, and the God of your understanding.

Jesus says further that God will reward us. The reward is that as we commune with God in our secret place, God is present to us. We then experience this "prayer-being," or "God with us" as Isaiah would say. This type of being overcomes the *persona*, or our "ego" or "self." Over time (remember the Buddhist monk to his meditations student) this will change us.

In the same Sermon on the Mount, Jesus says:

> Again, you have learnt how it was said to our ancestors: you must not break your oath, but must fulfill your oaths to the Lord.... All you need say is "yes" if you mean yes, and "no" if you mean no. Anything more than this comes from the evil one. (Matt 5:33–37)

Jesus is saying that as conversion takes place in our lives, what we say will flow out of our secret place, our true self. And when this happens, there will be great honesty in our speech. Our speech will be more direct. We will simply relate truthfully what we really are thinking and feeling inside. And we will not try to answer questions to which we do not know the answer.

The poet Matthew Arnold puts it this way:

> Only—But this is rare—
> When a beloved hand is laid in ours,
> When, jaded with the rush and glare
> Of the interminable hours,
> Our eyes can in another's eyes read clear,
> When our world-deafened ear

## A Conscious Endeavor

> Is by the tones of a loved voice caressed,
> A bolt is shot back somewhere in our breast,
> And a lost pulse of feeling stirs again;
> The eye sinks inward, and the heart lies plain,
> And what we mean, we say, and what we would, we know.
> A man becomes aware of his life's flow.[2]

Conversion happens on a daily basis as we practice rigorous honesty in assessing our lives. You will remember that earlier we mentioned that part of this conversion process includes making an honest assessment of our past.

We need to go back through all of the past influences in our lives (family, society, religion, teachers, friends, enemies, political beliefs, our prejudices, all of our "stuff") and one by one separate what we will keep and what we will discard.

We must not live in the past. That can destroy us. The purpose here is only to look at the past to understand deeply how it has molded us now. We then can forgive where we need to forgive (including ourselves), discard bad habits, keep the good ones, discard prejudices that exclude others, examine our intellectual approaches to reality, etc.

At the same time we will need to discover our own *personas*, and why we feel we need them to buffer us from the world and other people. Then we will slowly discard them.

In the end, we will become less *persons* and more *soulful*. Often when we want to compliment someone, we will say, "That Mary really has soul." What we are trying to say is that Mary is a very honest and direct person. What you see is what you get. There is no guile, no pretense, no ego. Mary is real.

Francis of Assisi was fond of saying, "We are what we are in the sight of God: nothing more and nothing less." As conversion progresses, our actions and words will more and more be in direct alignment with our innermost soul. They will flow out of our secret place.

But we must do more than examine our past and weed our gardens. We must also be able to place our minds and hearts in the presence of good things. This can happen through meditation, exercise, relationships with others, walks in nature, reading (poetry, literature, etc.) . . . there are many ways. But we must strive after experiences that help us to transcend ourselves and inspire us to lead what we consider to be a more elevated life.

2. Arnold, "The Buried Life," in *Works of Matthew Arnold*, 104–6.

## How Conversion Happens

In his novel *Don Quixote*, Cervantes credits a large part of Don Qhehana's transformation into Don Quixote to a thorough reading of all the extant literature on Knights Errant and Noblesse Oblige. There is an important relationship between the two. We must feed the soul if we want it to grow.

This conversion process is a unique journey for each of us. Thoreau speaks eloquently of these effects of conversion:

> It is something to be able to paint a particular picture, or carve a statue, and so make a few objects beautiful; but it is far more glorious to paint the very atmosphere and medium through which we look, which morally we can do. To affect the quality of the day, that is the highest of arts. Every man is tasked to make his life, even in its details, worthy of the contemplation of his most elevated and critical hour.[3]

As we change bit by bit, the little conversion that we have achieved becomes the measure for all of our actions. Our moments of conversion become the defining realities of our lives. These moments become the times when we discover most forcefully both who we are and what we are called to become.

---

3. Thoreau, *Walden*, in *Works of Henry David Thoreau*, 99–100.

# 4

# Reflections on Organized Religion and Biblical Inspiration

I HOPE THIS DISCUSSION will provide new ideas about the Judeo-Christian tradition, which contains much richness and depth of spiritual challenge. Sadly, this religious tradition seems an unattractive option because of the way it is often presented in its institutional framework, by various profession religious leaders, and by many who attend church and synagogue. G. K. Chesterton wrote:

> The Christian ideal has not been tried and found wanting. It has been found difficult and left untried.[1]

## A. ORGANIZED/INSTITUTIONAL RELIGION

It is important to put organized religion into perspective, since organized religion is most often to blame for representing the Judeo-Christian perspective so badly.

When I talk about the Judeo-Christian tradition (I was once challenged as to whether one can even use the term), I am referring to those traditions that arise out of the Old and New Testaments and have come down to us from Middle Eastern history and culture. The Christian religion has certainly introduced many traditions and beliefs that bear little if no relationship to Judaism. However, insofar as Jesus was profoundly Jewish, many of his teachings reflect the rich religious tradition out of which he

---

1. Chesterton, *What's Wrong with the World*, 5.

came. Many of his teachings, however—the most essential ones—are transcultural, and transtemporal.

Religious institutions play a different, albeit important, role as the backdrop to the vibrant life of reflective conversion I have described above. Active inner change may happen to people who affiliate themselves with a particular institutionalized religion, but sadly there is no necessary connection between the two. The major role of any religious institution should be to initiate and nurture the conversion process among its members.

Religions, or churches, are institutionalized expressions of particular teachings. As Emerson said it:

> An institution is the lengthened shadow of one man; as Monachism, of the Hermit Anthony; the Reformation, of Luther; Quakerism, of Fox; Methodism, of Wesley; Abolition, of Clarkson. Scipio, Milton called "the height of Rome"; and all history resolves itself very easily into the biography of a few stout and earnest persons.[2]

The purpose of religious, and truly of all, institutions is to preserve important teachings and values. Humans create institutions for everything important to them: religious beliefs, education, marriage, use of money (i.e., the bank system), government, etc. Institutions play an important human role of, hopefully, preserving what is best in our humanity. Institutions are meant to do something good. They can have an important role to play in our lives.

However, one of the many complexities of institutions of every brand is that the longer any particular institution exists, the more it "adds to," amends, and distances itself from its origins. Sometimes in good ways that help the institution adapt to present-day problems. But sometimes institutions become ossified and out of touch with present realities and needs. Institutional change is absolutely necessary, even though, paradoxically, most institutions resist change. For as time passes, history presents new events that demand new forms of understanding. For example, when money replaced the bartering system as a method of acquiring the necessities of life, the whole institution of economy had to rethink its relationships and how to determine value and the basis of trading one thing for another, from labor, to goods, to land, etc. This began to express itself in economic theories and practices, as well as in the creation of business and financial institutions.

---

2. Emerson, *Selected Writings*, 140.

## A Conscious Endeavor

Religion is another example of the necessity of changing to deal with new realities presented in historical time. Jesus did not live in a world that included genetic research, atomic and thermonuclear capabilities, corporate capitalism, or the rights of women in today's political sense. So not only does a religious institution need to deal with being historically distanced from the time and person of its founder(s), but religious institutions will find themselves faced with issues problems never posed during the time of its founder, but which challenge certain basic religious values in new and untried ways. How can the religious institution be sure it understands its spiritual values profoundly enough to be able to apply them to current situations in a way that leads people on a path to God through the present situations in which people find themselves? As I mentioned above, institutions resist change. Let us discuss the government of the United States as an example of institutional resistance to change. Once the American Revolution had occurred, and a federalist form of government was established, actual revolution against this new government was considered a heretical idea. Even though in Maryland, early on, there was a great need for land reform, and the citizens of Maryland in the 1790s came very near forming true revolution against the state of Maryland and the federalist government of the time. President Adams was fully ready to send federal troops to prevent such a revolution.

Very quickly, it seems, this fledgling government was resistant to revolution even though it was formed out of revolution. And so it has been ever since. One can cite examples of American history in which revolution was often proposed by various disenfranchised groups as a just response to their own oppression, from Native Americans, to black slaves, to the labor movement . . . the list could be rather long. But in every case, the United States government would absolutely resist the suggestion that one might have just cause to revolt against it.

And there is very little in our depository of revolutionary literature to which we can refer for reflections on the notion of an unjust government, and the rights of people to revolt against it. Other than the Declaration of Independence, writings by Thoreau, and Abraham Lincoln's first inaugural presidential address, there is very little mention of the right of revolution in extant American documents. We are always proud of the "American Revolution," or "the Whiskey Rebellion," or any past revolution. But for people to speak that way with regard to present injustices (many of which are quite more serious than a tax on tea) is judged as un-American and wrongheaded. Older revolutions become sacred the farther back in history they are situated. Our philosophical tradition in the United States has given us very few words concerning how to fertilize social change.[3] [4]

Max Weber, a nineteenth-century social philosopher, reflects on the social distancing of institutions from their founders in his book *Charisma and Institution Building*.

For Weber, forming institutions is part of human nature. Weber would almost describe man as *Homo institutionalis*. Humans form institutions to preserve some important aspect of their humanity. Institutions are meant to be good. They play an important role in preserving important functions and parts of what it means to be a human being. Weber describes in his writings the importance of the historical/institutional process. Weber wants us to understand how the historical process of institutionalization is initiated (usually by a charismatic individual or group), and how it evolves from a charismatic individual or group into becoming a movement. He later describes how, as "movements" develop beyond the region in which they are formed (and thinking their motivations are absolutely pure in wishing to preserve the values and insights of the movement), they begin to define an institutional reality with all the accretions, rituals, and baggage that institutions give birth to. Far from having a prejudice against institutions and the institutional process, Weber wants us to understand the historical process institutions do and must go through to remain vibrant enough to present their original charism to present historical time.

According to Weber, institutions are formed by charismatic individuals or by people who are the followers of a charismatic leader. The charismatic leader has introduced an idea, or way of life, or belief system. People gather around the charismatic leader, and what started as one person's way of life becomes a way of life for a small group of people. This small group of people remains pretty much a regional reality. But if they think the message of the original founder (s) is important enough, the group will begin to proselytize and move beyond the geographical region in which they formed themselves, bringing a message (insight) to other groups of people as well. As yet more groups form, what was once a small number of loosely related groups begins to take the form of a movement.

As a movement grows, it will spread even further beyond the geographical region and beyond the culture of the area where the original

---

3. Alinsky, *Rules for Radicals*, 7.
4. Ibid., 88.

charismatic leader lived. In doing so, the movement will begin to see the need to establish itself more firmly. At this point the followers may or may not see themselves to be establishing an institution. But leaders in the movement do see the necessity to set some things down in writing, perhaps rules of membership, modes of acceptable behavior, how to train new members (introduce them to the charism of the original founder). Ultimately, the movement will begin to form a structure with leaders. There will be positions of authority. All the while, as the institutional roles begin to form, those in positions of authority will see what they are forming as necessary to preserve the founder's charism. However, at times they might find themselves setting policies and establishing structures that seem to directly oppose the spirit of the original founder.

Let us take as an example the followers of St. Francis of Assisi in Italy in the thirteenth century. Within twenty years of the beginning of the Franciscan movement, leaders within the group were seeing the necessity to have control of, if not legally own, property and establish houses of study. Part of this was caused by the reality of a large number of clerics (priests) who were joining the movement. It was not long before Francis himself found it necessary to go to Rome and petition the pope to establish a religious order. As the order grew it established monasteries with a large membership. There were some in the movement who saw these developments as directly opposed to the original intent of Francis. Francis himself was in such confusion over some of the issues the movement had to deal with that he stepped down as its leader. But the movement continued to grow and became an institution known as the Franciscan Order, or Order of Friars Minor. One can imagine as one century passed, then two, and then three ... the changes with which this Order of Friars Minor had to deal. Some of the changes the order made were good and necessary. Some of the changes and adaptations the order made did put it in tension with its original charism. For instance, the more property the order controlled, the more power it had. There has always been a relationship between wealth and power. This power provided tensions that at times were destructive to the Franciscan charism.

The Order of Friars Minor is not unique in having to undergo this historical process and deal with this historical tension. At times preserving the order itself, its position of power in the Church and within secular society would seem to take on an importance totally divorced from the reason for which the order was established in the first place.

## Organized Religion and Biblical Inspiration

Let us take Christianity and the Catholic Church as another example of what Weber is trying to explain. Weber would say that while the question of whether Jesus himself intended to establish a church might have enduring and valid importance for church members, a church would have been established anyway because of *Homo institutionalis*. So for Weber whether Jesus intended to establish a church in our present day understanding is not as important as understanding how the Christian movement started, how it became a religion, and the forms it has taken. Weber would say we should understand historically how this movement behaved in its early days, how it moved out of Israel after the death of Jesus. Weber would be interested in examining how Christianity then had to deal with the general culture of the Roman Empire, how it had to later deal with more cultures as it spread, how it dealt with rejection, suspicion, success, position, power, and so on.

Weber describes how, in the process of going from a "movement" to an "institution," movements have to both organize and define themselves. As time moves on, the form of the institution will be continually molded by the historical situations which confront it and which it must confront. As the institution is separated by more and more years from the historical time of its founder, the institution in some senses takes on a life of its own. And in a very real sense this institution must find its way in the world. As this process unfolds, certain rituals and social behaviors become central to the identity of the institution. I will list a few of these in the case of Catholicism: sacraments, pope, bishops, priests, dogma, papal authority, etc.

Some of the institutional behaviors are good things. Some tend to lose their life-giving force over time, but may still be clung to. For instance, having church functions in Latin made very good sense at one historical moment in time, but eventually Latin became a stumbling block in many ways.

Or again, certain theological explanations about the universe made sense before Galileo, but these theological explanations made no sense once we knew for certain that the earth revolved around the sun.

Certainly belief in God and in Jesus Christ is something all Christians would say is a good thing, perhaps even the best thing on earth there is. But killing people for refusing to profess this belief, as happened in the Spanish Inquisition, is a bad thing.

Weber warns us that although institutions are good, institutions can take on behaviors, policies, and even beliefs that are bad.

I could give another example surrounding sports in the United States. Football is a particularly noteworthy example of something that has become an American institution. To trace the process of a sport becoming big business and the accompanying rituals and social behaviors that become part of it is interesting.

A case in point would be the Green Bay Packers. There was a time when the people of Green Bay formed a limited partnership and bought the franchise. It was really a team backed by the community. But as time has gone by, other people have been brought into the ownership (big money people), and the Packers have become just another professional football team.

As time passes and institutions take on lives of their own, they can get out of touch with the teachings of the founding charismatic leader. At the same time, the institution may be out of touch with present historical time. England has become famous for having many huge Anglican churches. They are beautiful but rarely attended. They are out of touch.

In Webers's view, when any particular institution has gone astray, but embodies values or teachings important beyond a particular culture or moment in history, then someone in a particular time will rise up within the institution. This person will be another charismatic leader in his/her own right, and will call the institution to renew itself and align itself with its founding charism.

For Weber, a few religious examples of this would be: (1) the prophets of the Old Testament, who reminded people of their need to convert their minds and hearts to God; (2) great religious leaders of the past who have helped to renew Christianity in their own time (Benedict of Nursia, Augustine of Hippo, Francis of Assisi, Therese of Lisieux) and by extension beyond Weber's time; (3) Pope John XXIII, who revolutionized the Catholicism of his day; (4) Mother Theresa of Calcutta, who called the world's attention to the plight of the poor.

These men and women who rise up from within the institution, according to Weber, call the institutional community back to the original intents and teachings of the founder(s), but in a way that speaks to the present historical time.

The appearance of the charismatic leader will often shake the institution to its roots and help it to change and fit the real needs of its time in a way that adapts the original founder's charism to the present historical time. The process Weber describes then begins all over again.

This has happened often in the religion we call Christianity. I will list the original charismatic leader as well as some subsequent charismatic leaders of later times in one column, and in the other those who have been the company men, the institution builders:

| Charismatic Leaders | Institution Builders |
|---|---|
| Jesus | Paul of Tarsus |
| Anthony of the Desert | St. Peter |
| Augustine of Hippo | St. John |
| Benedict of Nursia | The Popes |
| Francis of Assisi | Henry VIII |
| Claire of Assisi | Archbishop of Canterbury |
| Theresa of Avila | all bishops |
| Martin Luther | priests and ministers |
| John Fox | theologians |
| Thomas Merton | |
| Pope John XXIII | |
| Mother Theresa | |
| Dorothy Day | |

These lists are imperfect at best. Most people "tend" in one direction or another, but there are people who combine both charismatic and institutional gifts.

For instance, one need but read the letters of Paul to see that at times he could rise to levels of both philosophical and theological complexity. At other times he was a sublime poet. He was obviously a brilliant, charismatic man. But as history bears out, he was also a major leader in building the religious institution of Christianity.

When we look back historically we can see that in a very real sense he took the Christian movement and ran with it throughout the Roman Empire of his day. He was able to see even more clearly than Peter the importance of the Christian movement broadening itself to include more than converts from Judaism.

Paul realized how life is different when you are speaking, for instance, to people who have read Plato and Aristotle. So it is fair to say, within Weber's metaphor, that Paul was one who helped build Christianity as an institution.

## A Conscious Endeavor

Normally we use the term "charismatic" to refer to specific people. One does not speak of a charismatic priesthood, papacy, presidency, or other institutional office, although one might refer to a particularly charismatic priest, pope, or president.

Some people are tremendous charismatic leaders but terrible institution builders. Cesar Chavez (a man I greatly admired) was a charismatic labor organizer. But he had very little understanding of how to run a successful institution called a "labor union." He did not have the gifts to deal successfully with such necessary institutional realities and concerns as: ongoing labor contract negotiations, hiring halls and hiring hall policies, union membership issues, pension plans, health plans, etc.

In church institutions there are those who are good at building church buildings, schools, universities, retreat houses, etc. and being administrators (bishops and pastors). They are good at making sure the bills get paid and the lights go on when you flip the switch.

Others live lives of such deep commitment to God, like Mother Theresa, that they leave an imprint of the presence of God in their lives and times. Some do this in such a forceful way that they attract many others to God. These are the kind of men and women of which the poet Stephen Spenser wrote:

> I speak continually of those who were truly great,
> The names of those who in their lives fought for life,
> Who wore at their hearts the fire's center.
> Born of the sun,
> They traveled a short while towards the sun,
> And left the vivid air,
> Signed with their honor .

Every institution needs the administrator, the organizer, the manager, as well as the charismatic individual. Without both the institution will not survive in a way that relates its message in a contemporary and important manner, i.e., reveal the original insight and values to the present time.

The tension between the charismatic and institutional roles is a healthy one. Weber warns us that every institution must be careful that the preservation of the charism, and not the institution itself, is the institution's constant struggle. Yes, it is important to pay the bills and have the lights go on. The tragedy is if the lights go on and we discover the room is empty.

Understanding the historical process of institution building and accepting the process as normal can be liberating. This approach allows us to

## Organized Religion and Biblical Inspiration

affirm institutions and their roles in our lives without having an "America, love it or leave it" attitude. This approach gives us a perspective that allows us to accept the proper and good role institutions can and should play in our lives, while curing institutional errors, abuses, and shortfalls.

I have spent substantial time discussing our participation in institutional religion. At some point in our lives we need to move beyond the institutional experience of religion into the living realm of the spirit. When we live in the presence of the Spirit of God, true conversion begins to happen in our lives. And introducing us to the conversion of our hearts is purpose for which religious institutions exist. As Lao-Tzu said, "True leaders inspire people to do great things. And when the work is done, their people proudly say, 'See, we did it ourselves.'"

I make a distinction between what we call "religion" (the matter of institutional establishments), on the one hand, and "faith" (the living search for the presence of God by the individual (s) trying to convert him/herself) on the other. The goal of religious institutions is to encourage, lead people to, inculcate, and preserve faith. Religious faith is many things to many people. For me, besides being a living hope and trust in God, faith is a paradigm. By this I mean it is a system of beliefs, a perspective if you will, through and around which I create meaning in my life. Each of us has the task of making sense out of our lives. The religious perspective or "faith" is a choice one makes in order, among other things, to achieve meaning. Many people speak of faith as a gift, and there is certainly a gift quality to faith. But faith is also a choice. When two people get married, if they are going about it seriously, they have placed faith and trust in each other. While there are many gift aspects to this marriage relationship, in the main it is a choice we must make daily with our life partner. Some days, the rough days, we find ourselves making that choice many times. Religious faith is similar in its choices and commitments, except it is *the* primary and fundamental choice we make to centralize meaning in our lives. It becomes the hub of the wheel around which the spokes may be joined and without which one will never have a wheel to move in any direction.

This is not unusual. Many people we call philosophers have attempted to analyze human existence in ways to state meaningful explanations for our existence. The list is at least as long as the list in Walt Whitman's poem quoted in the Introduction. Often the areas of human existence they plumb with their questions can lead us to profound understandings of the human condition. Some philosophers have included the spiritual aspect of humanity as part of the area they ponder. But all of them, if they are true philosophers, do ask such questions as: Why is there something instead of nothing? What does life mean? Is there any meaning to our life, or are we just small parts in a huge mechanistic universe? What is death? Why are we here individually? Why does the human race exist? Are we just some fluke of evolution? What is our role as human beings on the earth? Is there a role for us? And the questions go on and on.

Every individual is tasked to understand why he/she is here and what is the meaning of his/her life. There are many perspectives that help us reflect on life and its meaning: art, religious belief, philosophy, science, literature, biology, chemistry, psychology, etc. Each offers a different approach to looking at human existence and human experience. All of them have their own validity and are not in conflict when they are revealing something that is true from the particular perspective they investigate. Truth *is*, and when any area of human investigation discovers something true, in a very real way it has risen to a deeper level where the truth discovered is bigger than the discipline that has discovered it. And when this occurs, that which is true from one area of investigation will never be in conflict with something that is true from another area of investigation. Apparent conflicts of truth are only because of our lack of ability to see right relationships in those instances.

Let us apply the metaphor of a vase on a stand in the middle of a room to illustrate the point I make. As I walk around the vase in the middle of the room, each step I take is going to give me a different view (perspective) of the vase. When I have walked half way round, I might see a picture drawn on the vase that was not visible from the other side of the room. Does this mean the picture I now see on the vase is the total vase, or that the picture I saw on the other side of the vase, and now no longer see from this side, no longer exists or has no validity? Of course not.

Let us now extend the metaphor and say the vase represents life, and a circle of human beings has situated themselves around the vase, each viewing the vase from a different perspective. Let us now give each of these people names: musician, painter, sculptor, poet, theologian, scientist, physicist, biochemist, geneticist, philosopher, botanist, environmentalist, politician, field laborer, father, mother, etc.

These different people have a certain experience of "life" (the vase) that has revealed a valid perspective to them insofar as it is something they have really experienced. All these people see something, but none sees the whole vase (all of life and all of life's truth).

## Organized Religion and Biblical Inspiration

So it is with the different disciplines or areas of knowledge we form with our minds to discover, interpret, and come to our understandings of what we call reality, or what is real, whether in a physical, emotional, intellectual, or spiritual sense. As we employ all these different disciplines and areas of knowledge, we must blend together many different perspectives into a continuum of meaning that works for us. It takes a whole lifetime to accomplish this, we are continually learning. As we get older, we begin to notice things about our life journey.

When I turned fifty, many people asked what being fifty is like. I responded that I liked being fifty because, "Having reached fifty I have learned that most of the time I know what I don't know; I realize that what I do know works for me but not necessarily for anyone else; I no longer find it important to try to convince anyone to my perspective; I find there are many people, cultures, and ideas I do not understand; and I find myself willing to be tolerant of practically anything except when another's behavior or belief does positive harm to others."

As a perspective, religious belief attempts to deal with some very big questions: Why are we here? How did we get here? Where are we going? How are we to behave towards each other? To the extent our belief system actually does this in a way that challenges us to positive moral growth, to right relationships with each other, or as Thoreau would say to help a person "elevate his life by a conscious endeavor," then it is doing what it is supposed to do.

In our own time religion has been criticized, often rightly, for not dealing with life questions in an authentic manner. These criticisms have taken the shape of "pie in the sky," "opiate of the people," and other rightly deserved descriptions. Religion often seems to relegate itself to some "other world," some spiritualized reality that does not relate to the life and problems humans see themselves facing right now.

At times the religious perspective has viewed life on earth as having little value, and therefore as not of too great a concern. Sort of a, "Hey, we're all gonna die anyway, so none of this is worth much consideration." Such religious perspective point out that our true home is some heaven off in the great beyond, in a next life. Often this has led to a moral lethargy and timidity regarding our involvement in the world.

This amazes me because the most famous men and women of faith we can think of—Jesus, Buddha, Mohammed, Theresa of Avila, and so many others—were fully involved in human life. They were people for whom compassion for others, a true expression of real concern for others, was very real. These great people were intensely interested in this life and how we treat each other while we are here. There are many stories told about how many of these people had the ability to heal people, to calm people, to give people new meaning for their lives. If this life does not matter that much, then it would make little sense for these people to be so involved in it. Thus, the measure of true faith is to be found in the extent to which it not only enters into our own lives and relates to a real conversion of the heart, but to how it involves us in the world intimately, helping us to create Right Relationships.

There is obviously much more that can be said about religion as an institution. We could mention historically many good and many evil things that have been done in the name of religion. This was not the purpose of our discussion. Our purpose was only to point out clearly the difference between religion, in an institutional sense, and our living faith on the other hand. When we understand the difference between the two, we can then intelligently evaluate what proper role, if any, each can or will play in our lives.

## B. BIBLICAL INSPIRATION

In addition to discussing religion as an institution, we need to discuss biblical inspiration. For like religion as an institution, how we understand the Bible, inspiration, and the scriptures of religious groups that are different from us (but whose revelation to them is as important as my understanding of revelation is to me—and just as valid insofar as they reveal truth) is important. In a Judeo-Christian context the whole reality of the inspiration of the Bible, and our understanding of this, can either help or hinder us as we apply the discipline of inner change or conversion in our lives and relationships. Again, we can think of this as clearing up some of the "inspiration stuff" in our lives.

From the time I was a young child I heard teachings and discussions about God inspiring the authors of the Scriptures. The idea that came into my head was one of God dictating to some apostle or prophet, who then took pen in hand and wrote it down. They were, in my mind's eye, more like transcribers or secretaries who faithfully took down God's dictation.

I no longer believe anything that even approaches that idea. I find it helpful when discussing biblical inspiration to discuss inspiration in the arts or sciences, in fact, all human inspiration. As we begin this discussion I want to be clear. I am not saying biblical inspiration and other forms of human inspiration are the same thing. However, when human inspiration in its truest sense deals with the discovery of some truth in a unique way, we can see similarities in all human inspiration. Clearly there are inspirations in different areas of human experience, and the truth they reveal may serve a seemingly different purpose. But all forms of inspiration that human beings experience have a common thread.

Let us look at musical inspiration in the life of Wolfgang Amadeus Mozart. Mozart was truly inspired. Inspiration has the quality of a gift. Certainly the inspired person has worked hard to attain a level of investigation or performance that allows them to "reveal" what is beautiful or true in human life. But even the inspired person, when having completed a work, realizes that what has occurred in his/her most inspired moments is a gift. Did Mozart hear the music in his head and then write it down? Did he agonize over its creation? Was he given a mental and emotional set of tools that allowed him to craft these magnificent works in ways that no one else could? Probably all of the above, and more.

What is interesting about the results of inspiration in any area of human life (religion, the arts, the sciences, etc.) is that whatever gift, or knowledge, or truth is given in inspiration *always* results in a product of some kind or an insight meant to be shared with all human beings. What is the use of writing music if it is not to be performed and heard? Why did Rodin sculpt and cast *The Thinker* if he did not plan for it to be seen? Once having discovered that the earth rotated around the sun, or that the world was round, this insight or knowledge would have been of little worth had it been kept hidden.

I am not saying an artist or any other person of great insight will have his/her talent or insight recognized and appreciated in his/her own lifetime. Some great people are recognized as such in their own lifetime. On the other hand, there are many who die in obscurity, and only later is their great work or their very life itself recognized for what it was.

Also interesting about inspiration is that the result or gift of inspiration always incorporates the personality of the creator, or in our example, the musician, artist, scientist, etc. There is something about the music of Mozart that is not Beethoven or Bach. There is something about Matisse that is not Renoir or Monet. One sees the handprints or character of the creator in the product.

Even though the resulting product of inspiration has the stamp of a particular personality or creator, it reveals something (a thought, an emotion, an experience of being) much more grand than the individual. We call this *beauty* or *truth*.

I am not speaking here of the little inspirations all of us receive in life, what some call the "Aha!" experience. Each of us gets small inspirations. We might be inspired to lose weight, or to be more patient, or to build a room on our house. These little inspirations happen, certainly, but they only relate to our individual lives, and do not have a grand consequence in the sense of being revelations for anyone else.

Let's look at an example of an inspiration that had grand consequences. One time at Sunday Mass, a priest, a Capuchin Franciscan, told the story of one of their missionaries in New Guinea.

Apparently the people of New Guinea have a very thorough understanding of "an eye for an eye, a tooth for a tooth." Truly they have added nuances to this that we would never imagine.

A friar was headed into the mountains to provide religious instruction in the villages. While traveling by jeep, he was stopped by some tribal members, robbed of everything but the shirt on his back, wounded with a spear, and left by the side of the road to die. Somehow he was able to make it on foot to a village where he was taken care of. Then he completed his work and headed home.

On his return home, he stopped at the place where he had been robbed. He began yelling for those who had robbed him to come and meet with him. Voices echo up and down the valleys since the mountain people communicate this way, enabling word to travel fast.

Two or three hours later the group of people who had been involved in the injury to him showed up. Instead of being angry with them and telling them how he was going to get even, the friar told them he forgave them. He added that he would like them to please not do to other people what they had done to him. He did not ask them to return what had been stolen. He did not ask them to join his religion. He simply forgave them. This is a good example of something we do that has grand consequences, that is bigger than us as individuals.

Truth is transcultural. When we live it, this becomes evident. The friar may have had some particular religious reasons to do what he did, i.e., he was trying to emulate the teachings of God. But he did not say, "I forgive you because God says I should forgive." He simply said, "I forgive you." The act of forgiveness is the most powerful act of all. This forgiveness introduced an alternative to the New Guinea people who had robbed him,

## Organized Religion and Biblical Inspiration

a new possibility in their relationships. Here is an example of an inspiration that had much greater consequences in the moral world. Again, as Thoreau would say, this friar was able to "affect the quality of the day." Any discussion about biblical inspiration and revelation is complex at best. But I think we can agree that when we try to define and understand biblical inspiration and revelation, we will find it has much in common with other types of inspiration we experience. Biblical inspiration is part of an inspiration continuum. Isolating biblical inspiration and revelation outside of this continuum creates constricted thinking and should make us suspicious.

What does biblical inspiration and revelation share with other types of revelation and inspiration, say, the artistic, intellectual, or scientific perspectives?

The poet Robert Browning once said, "A man's reach should exceed his grasp, or else what's Heaven for?" The most true or profound moments of insight that contain within them grand consequences that we experience in any endeavor (remember the vase and the different perspectives as ways we view and experience our world?) make us aware of something much greater than ourselves. This insight or experience at the same time will call greatness out of us, call us to a more profound humanity. It might be a scientific truth or insight. For instance, can you imagine what it must have been like for Jacques Cousteau when he finally understood the whole concept of environmental ecosystems and the interrelationships between salt water life, fresh water life, and human activity! Imagine how that must have challenged him to growth!

These experiences make us feel elevated, at one, in communion, or at peace. Even if our experience is from science, denotative language alone will not be able to define and relate the impact of the experience and its meaning in our life.

Such experiences have in common with biblical inspiration and revelation that they place us in the presence of a reality, a profound truth, that calls us to something much greater than ourselves. In fact, these experiences actually *are* experiences of a grand reality, and for some people, are actual experiences of the Divine in their lives.

The Mohammedans made great strides in science (particularly astronomy) in the eleventh through the thirteenth centuries. Their faith taught them that learning about the way the world works taught them about Allah at the same time. Thus to discover laws of nature was another way to learn about God. For them, a profound experience in understanding creation from a scientific perspective could be a profound experience of God at the same time.

Judaism and Christianity have held similar views as this. Ultimately, all inspiration dealing with any aspect of our complex lives *can be* a profoundly spiritual experience at the same time.

But how is biblical inspiration and revelation different? Scriptural revelation and the works that flow out of it (the Bible) have the overt intent of discussing a relationship between God and ourselves. The individual and/or faith group(s) out of which the Scriptures came already had made an assent to faith in God. Their inspiration was intended to reveal to all of us something important about what God is like, how God wants us to act, and what our reason for existence is in God's plan. While one might have a profound spiritual experience while viewing a particular painting or while hiking to the top of Mt. Everest, it is doubtful that the artist who created the work of art or the person who organized the expedition to Everest did so with a particular spiritual intent for those who would experience it.

Scripture has the unabashed intent and purpose of introducing the reader or listener to faith in God. All the Scriptures were finally written down in a particular time, culture, and language. The difficulty the writers of Scripture had is the same difficulty theologians and men and women of faith have today: How does one speak clearly about the infinite, all-loving God in limited human language and through our human limitations?

Thus we see the complexity involved with coming to an understanding of the writings we call Scripture. What is revealed in the Bible is both a word about God and a word about humanity. When Moses writes, he also reveals something about Moses, his culture, his prejudices, etc. For instance, if you read the Torah carefully, you will see that women and children are considered chattel. Is this revelation, or Moses reflecting his culture? Scholars would say the latter. The scriptural authors cannot but reflect their cultural strengths and weaknesses. Perhaps this is why the faith community and how it understands these works through time is of such great importance.

Obviously, the farther back in time we go, the more difficult it is to understand all the particulars of language, culture, historical events, that shaped the particular person(s) we are discussing. It is as difficult to know personal details about Moses as it is about Ramses II. Biblical scholarship has pointed out directions we might go. The list is not exhaustive, but minimally we can say that what biblical scholarship has discovered thus far certainly rules out a fundamentalist approach to Scripture.

I characterize the fundamentalist approach to be something like this: "I read it in my Bible. The Bible is God's word. Therefore, everything written in the Bible is absolute truth." Fundamentalist attitudes are not only unrealistic but have often been the cause of great human suffering. For instance, many racists use the language in Genesis 4 about the "mark of Cain" to justify their stupidity and racist behavior towards people of darker skin. We can safely say that such approaches have no place for the reflective individual.

In *The Music Man*, Profession Harold Hill has the whole town convinced he can teach boys and girls of the town to play instruments by using the "Think Method." The Think Method taught that all you have to do was think about the notes, and then you would be able to play them. Of course, in reality there was no Think Method, but peoples' belief in it allowed Professor Harold Hill to sell many musical instruments.

There are many religious hucksters who sell religion. They preach an instant salvation like my friend in the gas station so many years ago. All you have to do is accept Jesus as your personal savior and send a personal check to . . . The recent empires of Jimmy Baker and Jimmy Swaggart are excellent examples of the "Think Method" as applied to religion, as are many of the so-called sites of miracles such as Medjugorje in Catholicism. A healthy skepticism to these approaches is important. When a lot of money is exchanging hands in the name of religion, we should be immediately suspect.

Perhaps the biggest mistake the fundamentalist makes is that he places the Scriptures in a vacuum, as if they stand on their own apart from the faith community out of which they arose. A faith community that over centuries has had to grapple with the meaning of their faith, a community that has had to deal with its own contemporary issues and interpret for their time how the Scriptures speak to them in these various situations, is important in discovering what Scripture might mean for us today. Besides all the technical knowledge of language, culture, theology, history, anthropology, and so on that the scriptural scholarship community brings to the interpretation of Scripture, there is the faith of the community itself. The interplay of these is critical to a proper understanding of biblical inspiration and the nature of religious revelation. In fact, what we call the canon of the Bible today was determined by this faith community.

In order for you and me to have the beauty of Mozart revealed to us the way Mozart intended it, a whole group of men and women, including the conductor, must study music and their instruments for years. In addition, they must come to understand Mozart. Further, the conductor must understand the different instruments and how they are meant to blend together in Mozart's particular way. And even further, many instruments we have in today's orchestra were not invented when Mozart lived. The conductor and arranger of the symphony must be able to interpret what this means. This takes a long time. But because they are willing to do this, you and I can have the music and beauty of Mozart revealed to us today.

For us to assume that an understanding and appreciation of biblical revelation will not require the same commitment and discipline it takes to understand and appreciate Mozart is to fall back into the world of Professor Harold Hill's "Think Method." It simply doesn't work.

Biblical revelation is really intended for all people. This must at least mean that when it is presented to people, it must be presented in ways that give meaning to their lives and represent truths that are acceptable (not necessarily comfortable). These truths are not so complex they need to be placed in some technical theological jargon that is beyond the reach of people. If truth becomes purely esoteric, then it is of little value. If people of faith believed this, their approach would be different.

It can be quite difficult to separate the truths of Scripture from the cultural overlay and history of those who wrote them. This difficulty is intensified because the Scriptures arise out of an already existing religious movement that was in the nascent forms of an institution: Judaism or Christianity. The Scriptures are in many ways already an interpretation of the faith community out of which they arose.

With regard to the New Testament this reality presents a particular challenge for scholars who are searching for what Jesus might have said and taught apart from the faith community's interpretations.

Historically this has proven to be one of the most difficult tasks of any group of believers. For Christians, separating what Jesus taught from what Christians teach about Jesus has been perhaps one of the most agonizing and frustrating endeavors to be considered. Often the search for the "historical" Jesus is abandoned in frustration for lack of sufficient historical data. We find it difficult to find out what his actual words were and what he actually taught. But frustration is not a reason to abandon all attempts at such an understanding, especially if we want to be able to present to others what Jesus taught as a model, or a set of values for them to use in their lives.

## Organized Religion and Biblical Inspiration

Albert Schweitzer makes some very interesting observations regarding the quest for the historical Jesus. He would say that as far as its essential spiritual and ethical nature is concerned, Christianity's religious truth remains the same through the centuries. The variations belong only to the outward form that it assumes in the ideas belonging to different worldviews. Thus Jesus' religion of love, which made its first appearance within the framework of late Jewish eschatological (the end is coming!) expectation, finds a place later on within the late Greek, the medieval, and modern views of the world. What is decisive is the amount of influence over people won by the spiritual and ethical truth that it has held from the first. Jesus, for instance, never did require that people grasp in thought or speech who he was/is. He did not think it necessary to give those who actually heard his sayings insight into his innermost personality, nor to disclose to anyone his family tree. The one thing he did require of them was that they should actively and passively prove themselves to be men and women who had been compelled by God to rise from being of the world to being other than the world. The essence of the Judeo-Christian approach is an affirmation of the world that has passed through a rejection of the world. Within a system of thought that rejects much of what the world has to offer and teaches us to live life in view of death, it sets up an ethic of love and involvement.

There are some general principles I have formed for myself over the years after I have spent many years loving Scripture as a source of truth. I think one must also investigate biblical scholarship and related cultural and anthropological studies. As you have seen by now, I do not think we can look at the Scriptures uncritically. But as I have read and reread Scripture, searching out the values expressed there in order to find the living truth to which I can compare my own life and actions, I have come up a list of principles I apply as I approach Scripture that help me in separating revelation from the world of opinion, cultural influences, and particular institutional interpretations:

1. *Scripture does not try to define God.* Scripture does attempt to point out what God is like—God's desired and even real relationship to humans and to creation. Scripture tries to describe how we are supposed to relate to each other. Scripture uses connotative language in trying to discuss God's love for us. Scripture has more kinship with the connotative approach of great literature and poetry than it does with the denotative language of empiricism. I do not say this to degrade human ability to discover how nature operates through inductive

research and empirical approaches. But revelation is primarily a faith statement that God exists and that God is God and not human. Revelation about God will make clear that God's ways are not our ways. The greatest difficulty of all is talking about God while being limited to human language and expression. Such attempts at best limp, even in the Scriptures. But at the same time Scripture is formative of faith in that it is a body of writings by men and women who took their faith in God seriously, in fact, their discovery of God's presence in their own lives seriously. Many of these men and women had a great ability to write about what they had learned by their faith experience. When we look at the difficulties with education in our own time, the men and women of the world who wrote down what we today call the Scriptures evidence that they were highly educated people in their own time. Relatively speaking, there was greater illiteracy in biblical times than exists today. They have given us a body of writings that has inspired people to search for God seriously, and to take upon themselves lives of conversion more than they would ever have imagined.

2. *Scripture causes critical thinking/radicalism.* Revelation will always get to the root of things. What it will reflect upon will always be something that strikes at the core of some human problem about relationships, whether with God, humans, or creation. It will have no respect for conventionally or culturally accepted "truths" or the politics of the day. It will be neither "liberal" nor "conservative." These shallow political tags will prove meaningless in approaching revelation's radicalism.

3. *Scripture calls for personal conversion.* Revelation will always express a need for radical change from within the human soul.

4. *Scripture is not always comfortable.* Because of its radicalism and lack of conventional propriety, revelation stands up against popular perceptions of the day, be these personal, political, cultural, or religious perceptions about how the world ought to be. This is what John's Gospel is referring to when it says we are to be "in the world, but not of the world."

5. *Scripture appeals to our higher nature.* Revelation moves directly against things like greed, selfishness, materialism, and self-gratification, and suggests Right Relationships, elevated values, and a more ennobling way of life. As St. Augustine said, "Though the times be incredibly evil, live nobly, and you will change the times."

## Organized Religion and Biblical Inspiration

6. *Scripture demands rigorous honesty and truthfulness.* An English professor under whom I studied raised the question: What is a great novel, as opposed to an average to poor novel? His answer was that if one hundred years from now people are still reading it, you probably have a great novel in your hands. People want to continue to read great works of literature, because the great truths they discuss are trans-temporal and transcultural. The truths of revelation continue to inspire men and women to lives of great conversion. Their lives attract others in their time. Jesus still inspires people to lives of love and service. And Gandhi still inspires people to find non-violent solutions to social injustices.

7. *Scripture focuses on society's weakest members.* Who is the greatest? Revelation concerns itself with what happens to the little people, those without temporal or political power or wealth. Considering that at any particular time in history about 3 percent of the population controls 85 percent of the wealth, this should not be surprising.

8. *Scripture creates connectedness.* Revelation forms a faith community, not a bunch of individuals. Religious revelation will emphasize our relationships with God, others, and nature. Because of this, Scripture encourages us to be connected to others (the Good Samaritan approach to society), and appeals to us to form more inclusive communities based on love, justice, and service.

While this list is not exhaustive, it does point to what are some of the elements we can use in determining whether or not something we are reading in Scripture is divinely inspired. Armed with this and the traditions of the faith community, we can now turn our attention to the Old and New Testaments, and what attitudes they seem to convey about our place in the world, and how we are to share the goods of the earth.

# 5
# Old Testament Teaching Regarding Justice and Distribution

I WAS ONCE HAVING a discussion with my brother Mike, a professor of English literature at Cal Poly University in San Luis Obispo, California. He made a succinct and interesting comment. We were discussing some life questions and he said, "Hey, once you know who and what you are, everything falls into place." He is right.

As we begin a walk through the Old Testament, we very quickly come to an understanding of who those writers thought they were in God's eyes, and why we are here.

It is clear the Old Testament expresses belief in a God who is the creator. It is clear the Old Testament expresses belief that there is only one God. God is totally other. But at the same time, the God of the Scriptures seem to have created in such a way that God reveals himself in creation, and somehow the message seems to be that even those who exist today—people, trees, neutrons, all of it—are the result of that ongoing creation. The various books of the Old Testament, after expressing this belief, talk at length about what our response to God as creator ought to be. We are to acknowledge the existence of God, and we are to have an obedient attitude. We are somehow to "obey" God.

It is helpful when talking about obedience to God, to first just look at the word itself. The word *obedience* comes from the Latin verb *obaudire*. *Ob-* is a prefix that means "to," and *audire* is a verb that means "to listen." When you put the two together you have "to listen to." An obedient person, then, is one who listens to another. The obedient person is an active listener.

# Teaching Regarding Justice and Distribution

Have you ever talked with someone and felt they were five hundred miles away? Have you ever "listened" to another person and noticed that instead of really listening you were thinking of what your answer was going to be, or wishing they would hurry up so you could get on to your next appointment or experience? Perhaps what you really want to do is set this other person straight, "fix" his/her problem. Of course, this in not real listening.

On the other hand, have you ever seen a baby look at you? They look at you with absolute and full attention. Or have you ever been in the presence of someone who gave you their full attention? Perhaps they gave you full eye contact the whole time you were talking. They didn't look at their watch. They gave you the feeling there was absolutely nothing else they would rather be doing than listening to you. Giving this full attention is "listening to." This constitutes true obedience. The person who gives you their full attention is obedient in their attitude towards you. What the Buddhists talk about when they teach meditation is a form of active listening, and leads to union with God.

The person who is searching for an understanding of God is like that. He/she is constantly listening, searching, groping. The attitude of listening is very important to a person of faith.

The Old Testament gives us glimpses of who God is. In Psalm 47, the psalmist expresses it succinctly: "God is king of the whole world" (47:7). By using a metaphor of his own time that people would readily understand (kings had the power of life and death over humans; what greater power is there in earthly terms?), he extends that metaphor to God showing that his power is not just regional, but over all creation. And who are we? Psalm 39 is clear:

> You have given me an inch or two of life. Each man that stands on the earth is only a puff of wind, each man that walks, only a shadow; and the wealth he amasses is only a puff of wind—he does not know who will take it next. (Ps 39:5–6)

We are just passing through. Francis of Assisi used to say, "We are only Pilgrims and Wanderers." A lot of "things falling into place" begins with the realization of death. Each of us is going to die. There is no avoiding the issue. We will die.

When Thoreau said "the mass of men lead lives of quiet desperation," he at first seems to be referring to our day-to-day neuroses, our "hustle and bustle" attitude towards life, our always being in a rush to make money or do some project. I am referring to here what Rinpoche earlier described when he spoke about how we give so much time to what we see as our "responsibilities," and that we should perhaps be calling them our "irresponsibilities" insofar as they keep us from leading lives of true reflection and inner peace. But what Thoreau is really referring to is our fear of death, our frantic avoidance of dealing with our mortality. We just don't want to think about death. We find it scary and depressing. We are afraid of death. We are angry about death. We don't understand death.

So instead of dealing with death head on, we avoid even thinking about death. We divert ourselves. We divert ourselves with all the power of our being. We create and become involved with what we can then consider to be serious considerations and responsibilities: acquiring, having, controlling, inventing. We create businesses, economic kingdoms, even families, in some frantic attempt to make a mark that says we were here. The Buddhists say we should be living our lives as a preparation for death. We avoid this approach.

We become involved instead in power. We seem to think the power we might gain by financial successes will give us power over death, that it will give us some sense of immortality, something that will remain after we are gone. William Wordsworth describes the process of becoming more involved in "worldly things" as we lose our perception of the spiritual in this manner:

> —But there's a Tree, of many, one
> A single Field which I have looked upon,
> Both speak of something that is gone:
> The Pansy at my feet
> Doth the same tale repeat:
> Whither is fled the visionary gleam?
> Where is it now, the glory and the dream?
>
> Our birth is but a sleep and a forgetting:
> The Soul that rises with us, our life's Star,
> Hath had elsewhere its setting,
> And cometh from afar:
> Not in entire forgetfulness,
> And not in utter nakedness,
> But trailing clouds of glory do we come
> From God, who is our home:
> Heaven lies about us in our infancy!
> Shades of the prison-house begin to close
> Upon the growing Boy,

## Teaching Regarding Justice and Distribution

> But He beholds the light, and whence it flows,
> He sees it in his joy;
> The Youth, who daily farther from the east
> Must travel, still is Nature's Priest,
> And by the vision splendid
> Is on his way attended;
> At length the Man perceives it die away,
> And fade into the light of common day.
>
> Earth . . . doth all she can
> To make her Foster-child, her inmate, Man,
> Forget the glories he hath known,
> And that Imperial palace whence he came.[1]

Thus in our life, which is "a sleep and a forgetting," we lose ourselves in our consumptive and acquisitive life. If we get and control enough material "stuff," we also enjoy the power that comes with it.

But when all is said and done, our ideas of power and ownership are almost laughable when compared to the power of God expressed in Psalm 24:

> To Yahweh belong the earth and all it holds, the world and all who live in it. (Ps 24:1)

If one must talk about power and ownership, these words and the notion expressed in them are humbling. The psalmist is expressing in human terms that if the richest person in the world were to look at all he "owns" and then compare that to God, it isn't really ownership at all. We will die. And as I said before, this is humbling. And that is exactly what the psalmist's word are meant to be: humbling. Humility is a scriptural virtue.

Often we do things to belittle each other. We inappropriately call this "humbling" someone else. The adjective and noun "humble" and "humility" come from the Latin *humilis* and *humus*, which means "earth" or "dirt." A humble person never forgets that he/she is made of dirt and dust, and will return to dust when he/she dies. A humble man/woman lives his/her life staring death in the face. Every act is done in a way that is related to death.

I am not speaking of some macabre or obsessive idea of death. I call it a "healthy realization of our mortality." There are many things in our lives that would be put in their proper perspective if we stopped and thought for a moment, "Wait a minute, I might be dead by tomorrow, so how important is this really?" On the other hand, there are many things in our lives

---

1. Wordsworth, "Ode on Intimations of Immortality," 509–15.

we would value much more highly if we remembered we could be dead tomorrow. Part of the task we have is to not let our lives be "a sleep and a forgetting." The reflective person keeps death on his/her mind because it allows him/her the proper attitude of humility in all his/her relationships. Such a view will certainly color our relationship to our acquisitiveness, to our spouse, children, friends, indeed, all our relationships. If we really lived our lives as if we had only six months left to live instead of sixty years, we would focus our energy on those aspects of human life and experience that are truly important. Thus, humility is not God putting us down. Humility is simply realizing we are creatures of God, and not trying to be who we are not.

When I say the Scriptures talk about a creator God, I am not saying the Scriptures claim to know how or when this creation took place. Certainly the accounts of Genesis (there are two separate creation accounts in Genesis) draw on popular creation myths of the time.

A lot of mental and emotional energy has been wasted by people who argue about creation as expressed in the Bible (whatever that means, usually some "think method" approach) and evolution. The Scriptures are not a science book, and those who try to employ them as such might as well try to drive a car from Los Angeles to Hawaii. That doesn't work either. In both cases you are "all wet."

Science operates by inductive and logical reasoning, and forms "hypotheses" and "theories" that try to explain the complexities of how what we call "physical" reality operates. It tries to discover relationships between physical bodies, ultimately going from the macro world of bodily relationships to the micro world of particle and wave theory. Let me give you a more simple example. From about 400 BC to about 1500 AD, the scientific view was that the earth was the center of the universe. With all the best tools of observation, the scientific inductive method accepted this theory as "fact," and religious people developed theological theories that were compatible with this world view. As human scientific skills developed and grew, Copernicus invented the telescope, and Galileo published some new information based on his observations with this new piece of equipment, including basic mathematical calculations. A new theory was developed to explain the movement of the heavenly bodies. The new theory was earth-shaking, literally, and Galileo was condemned by the world of religion as a heretic for making conclusions based on his observations. His conclusions and new theory were at odds with existing scientific and theological

## Teaching Regarding Justice and Distribution

theories of how the world operated. His theory would require a new way of thinking and operating, and humans just did not want to do that. It is never comfortable to have to re-examine all your assumptions about life. Robert Frost expresses this resistance to truth very well in his poem "Birches," in which he forms one of the most beautiful meditations about life from reflecting upon boyhood memories about swinging on birch tree branches:

> But I was going to say when Truth broke in
> With all her matter of fact about the ice storm

There are some aspects of truth that truly come crashing into our lives and make our lives forever different, whether we want to acknowledge the truth facing us or not. There are many times "truth" makes us extremely uncomfortable. When St. Augustine became aware of the "truth" revealed to him about his own life and his need for inner change, his famous repine was, "Lord, convert me . . . but not yet!"

Science operates the way it is supposed to, by forming theories that have enough data backing them up to make them plausible, and that works as a mental construct to explain our relationship to "physical" reality. Evolution is another such theory. It seems helpful in explaining some of the realities we experience in the world. As such it can be a helpful theory. Evolution theories have never made the claim to explain everything. But evolution is helpful in piecing together what we observe from field experience in archaeology and other forms of scientific examination of our human history.

But let us suppose we some day discover how creation actually took place empirically, and that it is much more complex than the facts evolution explain. Then a new theory will be put forth that will be as earth shaking as the theory of Galileo in its time, or Darwin's observations in his time. We must anticipate being shaken as part of our journey to self-knowledge and world knowledge.

Remember the vase in the middle of the room? The scientist is looking at reality in one way. The religious perspective is looking at it in another way. They simply see reality from different (not necessarily opposing) perspectives. The realities are not in conflict. Those who insist they "must" be in conflict do not understand the universality of truth.

The scriptural perspective about a creator God is simply that at some point God created something that has resulted in us here and now. Biblical creation stories do not teach us science, but present to us the proper attitude of humility.

How that happened is unimportant in relation to the questions: "Who are we?" and "Why are we here?" What is important is our realization that we and every other person, and what we call animals, plants, minerals, atoms, electrons, energy—all are creatures of God as much as us. All are fellow creatures. "The soul that rises with us, our life's Star, hath elsewhere its setting, and cometh from afar." It is essentially this notion, which Wordsworth so well expresses, that is the Judeo-Christian basis for the dignity of all human beings, and all of creation.

Let us discuss this notion of our creatureliness. The word "creature" comes from the Latin *creatus*, which means "created." We are creatures. We are here. We will die. God is God. This is the attitude of humility to which we are introduced. We are not God. We are God's creatures. We have a place, a purpose. There is a specific relationship we have within this great creation to all other creatures. We are here to live out that relationship.

What was this relationship meant to be from the beginning? Usually discussions of this topic begin with the Book of Genesis and the creation accounts. They start here not because these accounts were written first. We know they were not. We start here because these creation accounts attempt to deal with our beginnings.

In the creation accounts there is a discussion about men and women and everything else being created, and then there is a discussion about naming all the other creatures. In his novel *Bound for the Promised Land* Richard Marius describes the voyages of a Virginia youth named Adam who heads to the American West in the nineteenth century to search for his father. His father had gone West like so many others to seek his fortune and then send for his family. Adam's mother died soon after his father's departure. Adam decides to travel West to find his father—an epic journey for a sixteen-year-old youth. He meets a mountain man and travels with him for a while before he finally asks the man his name. He quickly finds out that it is not proper mountain man etiquette to ask a man's name. The mountain man responds to Adam:

> Well, I mean, a name's a personal thing. It ain't something you want people to take like nothing, you know. Your name . . . Give somebody your name, you give him the power to make you turn around any time he calls it, like you had a string tied on your nose. And he had a hold on the other end. Maybe a nobody. A little runt with spit for a brain.[2]

---

2. Marius, *Bound for the Promised Land*, 149.

# Teaching Regarding Justice and Distribution

Aristotle claimed that the ability to name something meant that we understood its essence. For instance, we can look at several different types of horses (Palominos, Quarter Horses, Arabians, Morgans, etc.), and see certain things about them that are in every case applicable to horses in general (their essence). All the different breeds share some things in common which want us to call them all horses, and not cows or something else.

We do the same with windows, chairs, trees—literally everything. When we name something, we know its essence. This is an important insight.

In the creation accounts in Genesis, Adam and Eve are given the instruction to name things. Clearly the scriptural attitude is that human beings have the ability to understand the relationships of things, to know their essence, and the scriptural story encourages us to make these discoveries in our development of knowledge about reality.

But as the mountain man above states, knowing the name, the essence, brings with it power. When science figured out certain ways the atom functions this knowledge brought with it a terribly destructive power, in the form of the atom bomb, which we have been trying to curb ever since. On the other hand, there are probably peaceful uses for fission and fusion, which could make this knowledge worthwhile.

There does not seem to be an inference from Scripture that men and women are meant to do whatever they want with the knowledge they discover. The scriptural attitude does not encourage an attitude that expresses itself as: "Because I can do X, I should do X." It is good to know you can do X; otherwise you cannot exercise freedom, wisdom, and a proper moral attitude towards the universe. We are clearly here to understand the relationships between things, each other, and God. But, as Thoreau would say, we are here to live an elevated life through a conscious endeavor.

Those who resist scientific advances in knowledge because they have not been able to relate scientific perspectives to religious or other perspectives seem to be reacting out of fear. As human beings we should be trying to fully understand our human situation with all the God-given abilities and tools we have available for attaining knowledge. However, we should do so with humility, not pride.

In the Genesis story, words like "dominion" and "subjugate" are used. "Dominion" is a derivative of the Latin *dominus*, which means "Lord," one of the names we use for God. Perhaps the idea expressed in having dominion over creation is to treat creation as the "Lord" would. Again, we use the phrase "to lord it over someone" to describe someone who abuses his/

her power. But if we truly want to be imitators of the Lord in our "lording over" of creation, we will change our attitude. We will have the attitude of humility in our relationship to earth.

In the scriptural perspective, we are here to treat creation just like God would. We are not to behave as if God does not exist, and therefore do whatever we wish to our fellow creatures. We are to understand the relationships, see their essences, and put a name to them as we understand them, which allows us to live in Right Relationship to them.[3]

The Genesis stories seem to make clear that attempts to control nature are going to be difficult. When one thinks of the tasks one must do to subjugate someone else, one realizes how difficult and undesirable the subjugation relationship is from both the perspectives of the subjugator and the subjugated. One need only look at the American treatment of the indigenous peoples and of Africans brought as slaves to this land to understand what I am talking about. Just as humans find it distasteful and even hateful to be treated as less than they are, so too does all creation. As we have seen through the development of the field of ecosystems, all creation reacts negatively to abuse. The Genesis story does encourage humans to treat creation in a subjugating manner. It merely suggests the already existing fact that humans do try to subjugate the earth and each other.

The story of the Garden of Eden does not so much express what humanity fell from, but more rightly suggests what it is like when people live in Right Relationship with God and with each other. When this happens, life is a Garden of Eden. Jesus will later talk about this using the expression "Kingdom of God." In both cases, the Garden of Eden and the Kingdom of God are inside us. "Garden of Eden" and "Kingdom of God" express an inner spiritual attitude about relationships that can flow out from our souls. And when this attitude flows out of us, Right Relationships can exist. When these Right Relationships exist, things like shame and selfishness are curbed, and a better humanity is expressed.

The Ten Commandments (Exodus 20) have been taking rather a beating these days. However, if one looks at them in relation to the use of the world's goods, they are fairly straightforward directives that, if obeyed, would

---

3. Our naming of things and our understandings evolve and grow. Sometimes we name things wrongly, as when people in Europe believed the earth was the center of the universe till the fifteenth century. Often our wrongly naming of things is not malicious. For example, when DDT was invented it was hailed as a great product for insect pest control. It was not till years later that Rachel Carson was able to demonstrate to us its terrible destructiveness to our environment and the whole ecological cycle of life.

## Teaching Regarding Justice and Distribution

certainly enhance Right Relationships in any society. Acknowledge God above all else. Do not worship material images (one could even say the god materialism). Honor your parents. Don't kill. Don't commit adultery. Don't steal. Don't lie. Don't be avaricious about what your neighbor has. Moses, having been raised in the house of a pharaoh, would have had the best education Egyptian society of his day had to offer. He certainly would have been trained in things like the legal Code of Hammurabi, and other basic legal structures of his time. His Ten Commandments lay down the very basic rules by which a society must organize itself if it is not going to live in chaos. For any worldview that is going to encourage human beings to be stewards of the earth, to discover the essence of things and their proper relationships, there are some very basic things you must not do in order to stay on a positive path. The Ten Commandments express these basic rules of humanity.

The Old Testament holds the view that part of being human is to be a steward. Humans have created property ownership to place stewardship within a societal/legal/inheritance framework. Therefore the reason for ownership is not so we can become involved in materialism. Rather, it is so we can exercise our stewardship. Each of us needs to learn how to care for the earth. Ideally, we should be able to share the whole earth. However, historically we have not been willing to do this. As a result, we have created legal structures of ownership by individuals (property and assets) and groups (towns, cities, states, nations). Lack of ownership excludes many from the experience of stewardship, save in our national parks. If we cannot exercise stewardship, then an important aspect of what it means to be human is kept from us, and the experience of nurturing does not grow in us as it otherwise might.

I cannot stress this enough. Years ago I was working as a Catholic chaplain in the Los Angeles County jails (with approximately ten thousand inmates). A program was started allowing some of the prisoners to grow a garden. Inmates learned valuable things about nurturing plants that taught them in turn a lot about life. Thoreau ponders in *Walden Pond* about the raising of a garden and about green peas in particular. He reflects about the different stages of the growth of the peas—what weeds and bugs he has to look out for in order to assure the growth of the peas. He then pondered, as only Thoreau could, how he needed to nurture certain things within himself to assure that they too would grow—such qualities as patience, care, and attention.[4] Thoreau also noticed how the same things that nurtured the plants

---

4. Thoreau; *Walden*, in *Works of Henry David Thoreau*, 183–84.

nurtured him and the fellow creatures who lived with him at Walden Pond, and that really the whole earth should be equally cultivated like a garden.

There is something about our relationship to the earth that is important for us to learn. It seems this cannot be learned if we are not given a part of it to nurture. Many of the prisoners who were in the gardening program learned skills while gardening that were transferable to their family lives: watchfulness, patience, consistency, nourishment, nurturing, and attention.

In the Old Testament, justice is tied to ownership. When one has justice, he/she will own some land. In a society in which people do not own land, then to that extent justice is lacking.

It is noteworthy that as one looks back through history many basic human rights have often been tied to the ownership of land: citizenship, voting rights, rights of occupancy, etc. We need to pay attention to this notion because ownership in many ways has been the basis of much of our Western tradition of law and human rights. In fact, in Western thought, women and children had no rights until they were finally seen as humans and not the property of a man.

But a more important notion we must also keep in mind is that in the Judeo-Christian traditions prior to the idea of ownership is stewardship. Our stewardship arises out of our dignity as sons and daughters of God.

The scriptural approach does not reduce itself to the lowest common denominator. It often looks for the common or utilitarian good, but more often for an absolute moral good. People are often afraid to discuss the idea of moral absolutes in a world where tolerance is the norm. But Scripture does deal in very basic moral absolutes. Scripture states that there is a basic justice all must have, or we do not have a just society. The scriptural teaching starts from this same place: there is a God; God created; we are stewards.

After the Ten Commandments are given, the writer of Deuteronomy does not have God say, "If you don't do these things, I will send you to hell when you die." The writer has God say that people who keep these commandments will be blessed by peace within their borders. This is the gift that justice brings. If we read the Ten Commandments carefully, we will begin to understand that the effect of morality is a here-and-now thing, not something that gets rewarded only when we die. When we create Right Relationships now, both we and the whole earth benefit right now!

Remember earlier when we were saying that the Garden of Eden and the Kingdom of God are inside us? Inside us, written in our hearts, is where the Ten Commandments are meant to be as well. If we are trying to convert

## Teaching Regarding Justice and Distribution

ourselves to the good, the blessing is here and now, in the sense that our relationships with others will be Right Relationships as all of us strive to live a nobler life. All society benefits from the endeavor of one person to live a higher life.

There are some other sections of the Old Testament that I am going to cite in rapid succession, because taken all together they convey an Old Testament attitude about compensation, use of the world's goods, profits, charging of interest, and taking care of someone when they are not able to work:

> If men quarrel and one strikes the other a blow with stone or fist so that the man, though he does not die, must keep his bed, the one who struck the blow shall not be liable provided the other gets up and can go about, even with a stick. He must compensate him, however, for his enforced inactivity, and care for him until he is completely cured. (Exod 21:18–19)

> You must not molest the stranger or oppress him, for you lived as strangers in the land of Egypt. You must not be harsh with the widow or the orphan. . . . If you lend money to any poor man among you, you must not play the usurer with him: you must not demand interest from him. (Exod 21:20–25)

> For six years you may sow your land and gather its produce, but in the seventh year you must let it lie fallow and forgo all produce from it. Those of your people who are poor may take food from it, and let the wild animals feed on what they leave. (Exod 23:10–11)

> You must not exploit or rob your neighbor. You must not keep back the laborer's wage till the next morning. . . . You must not be guilty of unjust verdicts. You must be neither partial to the little man nor overawed by the great; you must pass judgment on your neighbor according to justice. (Lev 19:12–15)

> When you gather the harvest in your country, you are not to harvest to the very end of your field, and you are not to gather the gleanings of the harvest. You are to leave them for the poor and the stranger. I am Yahweh your God. (Lev 23:22)

What we are beginning to get a glimpse of in the first few books of the Old Testament (the Torah essentially lays down rules of social and religious life in the Judaism initiated under Moses and Aaron) is the concept of distributive justice. Distributive justice tries to get at how to distribute the goods of the earth in the most fair manner. While we discuss this idea we will have to keep in mind the Old Testament social milieu in which women and children could not own property and therefore had no rights. As a matter of fact, they were handled as property or chattel. Their status was totally derived from their relationship to the male member of society to whom they were attached. One can certainly not defend this worldview today, but one can see that if the concept of distributive justice as called for in the Torah were carried out, no one would be in want, no one would be poor.

The Old Testament attitude has very serious ideas about the poor. The poor are called the *anawim*, which means "God's poor." Why are they God's poor? The widow and the orphan do not belong to (are not the property of) anyone, so they have no one to turn to but God. The poor are called such because their plight cries out to heaven for justice.

In the Old Testament ideal an oppressive social pyramid occurs only when God's laws are not being obeyed. This leads to class inequities with the poor being victimized by the predatory rich. The prophets, whom we will discuss later, wax eloquent on this issue.

In the Old Testament the poor, the widow, and the orphan are the *anawim*. These are the powerless people of Old Testament society. Men might be poor or powerless because they do not own land. Widows and orphans are powerless because, considered as property, they are not owned by a man, therefore no one is responsible for their welfare. These situations cry out to God for justice because these people have no one else to turn to.

The Old Testament judges society by referring to the poor, the orphan, and the widow as a barometer of distributive justice. If they are being taken care of, then society is obeying God's law. If you own things, you are to administer them in a way that leaves something for the poor, the orphan, and the widow. You are not even to charge interest on loans to the poor.

It is interesting that today banks give preferred interest rates (called the Prime Lending Rate) to the wealthy, while the poor seem to always be paying the higher rates. I understand the reason the banks give—that the poor are a higher risk—but it was not the poor who bankrupted taxpayers in the 1980s when the Savings and Loan Crisis occurred in the United States. In other words, we need to reflect on our lending practices and examine whether or not the assumptions they are based upon are true on the one hand and just on the other. How risky is it really to lend to a poor man?

Further, the evolution of the banking industry into bigger and bigger banks with less staff and less personal contact with consumers has led to a

## Teaching Regarding Justice and Distribution

less personalized system and a de-emphasis on community lending. Often people are reduced to a computer formatted credit report that tells nothing about the personal integrity of the consumer. It is a difficult enterprise for those who are lower middle class or poor to work with the banking system to initiate potential business ventures.

The whole process of proper use of the goods of the earth ties back into the idea of conversion. Society's health is directly related to converting our minds and hearts to God. That *is* the Old Testament view.

Nowhere is this more dramatically seen than in the observation on the Year of Jubilees expressed in Leviticus 25.

In the Judaism that grew under Moses, the number seven was an interesting and important number. Every seventh day was a Sabbath day, every seventh week a Sabbath week, every seventh month a Sabbath month, every seventh year a Sabbath year. After seven Sabbath years (seven times seven, or forty-nine years) came the fiftieth year, which was designated the Year of Jubilees. The Year of Jubilees was referred to as "the acceptable year of the Lord" or the "year of the Lord's favor." During the Jubilee Year the following occurred:

- The land was redivided. If you had none, all of a sudden your patrimony was returned.
- All debts were forgiven.
- All slaves were freed.
- All prisoners were released.

An interesting line from Leviticus describing the Year of Jubilees says:

> Land must not be sold in perpetuity, for the land belongs to me, and to me you are only strangers and guests. (25:33)

This last phrase is a very powerful statement—"You are only strangers and guests." Have you ever been a guest in someone's home? Have you noticed how you do not make presumptions about what you may or may not do, but you treat your host and his/her wishes with respect? We need this same attitude in our relationship to the world and its goods.

At the end of the description of the Year of Jubilees, these words are put into the mouth of God:

> If you live according to my laws, if you keep my commandments and put them into practice, I will give you the rain you need at the right time; the earth will give its produce, and the trees of the

> countryside bear their fruits. You shall thresh until vintage time and gather grapes until sowing time. You shall eat your fill and live secure in your land. I shall give peace to the land, and you shall sleep with none to frighten you. (Lev 26:3-6)

The Year of Jubilees states most radically and forcefully the social value of distributive justice. Societies are most at peace when there is the greatest distributive justice. I do not mean by this that every person has exactly the same amount of material ownership. But at the same time it is clear that if distributive justice prevails, everyone will have what they need. Everyone will be able to exercise stewardship and thus live out one of the sacred roles given by God. Stewardship is a sacred trust that makes us all more human.

The realities of starvation, war, and disease are more often than not directly related to people not having a sufficient livelihood to take care of themselves and their families.

This is why it is clear that if we want peace we must work for justice. Until we become convinced in a very fundamental way (both personally and politically) of this direct relationship between just distribution of wealth and peace, peace will remain elusive.

Of all the Old Testament writers, the prophets are most concerned about the meaning of justice. Whenever the existing king was not making sure that the distributive justice of the Year of Jubilees was being carried out, a prophet would appear. He would always call the king and the nation to conversion.

Isaiah expresses this faith attitude most poetically and poignantly:

> Shout for all you are worth
> Raise your voice like a trumpet.
> Proclaim their faults to my people.
> Their sins to the House of Jacob.
>
> They seek me day after day,
> They long to know my ways,
> Like a nation that wants to act with integrity,
> And not ignore the law of its God.
>
> They ask me for laws that are just,
> They long for God to draw near;
> "Why should we fast if you never see it,
> Why do penance if you never notice?"

## Teaching Regarding Justice and Distribution

Look, you do business on your fast days,
You oppress all your workmen;
Look, you quarrel and squabble when you fast,
And strike the poor man with your fist.

Fasting like yours today
Will never make your voice heard on high.
Is that the sort of fast that pleases me?
A truly penitential day for men?

Is not this the sort of fast that pleases me
It is I God who speaks—
To break unjust fetters
And undo the thongs of the yoke,

To let the oppressed go free,
And break every yoke,
To share your bread with the hungry
And shelter the homeless poor,

To clothe the man you see to be naked,
And not turn from your own kin?
Then your light will shine like the dawn,
And your wound be quickly healed over.

Your Integrity will go before you
And the glory of God behind you,
Cry, and God will answer,
Call, and God will say, "I am here."

If you do away with the yoke
The clenched fist, the wicked word,
To give your bread to the hungry,
And relief to the oppressed.

Your light will rise in the darkness,
And your shadows become like noon,
God will always guide you,
Giving you relief in desert places.

God will give strength to your bones
And you shall be like a watered garden,
Like a spring of water,
Whose waters never run dry.

## A Conscious Endeavor

> You will rebuild the ancient ruins
> Build up on the old foundations,
> You will be called "Breach Mender," And "Restorer of Ruined Houses."
> (Isa 58:1–12)

I have quoted Isaiah at length because, as I said, he so beautifully captures the Old Testament prophets' approach. Notice that the rewards of justice are not off in some far away heaven. The prophet is always clear to point out that there are real benefits now for all society as each of us makes a conscious endeavor to manage the goods of the earth in such a way that the needs of all are met.

It is clear that the Old Testament perception is one in which God owns and we are his stewards. We are to take care of the earth as though it belongs to someone else, and to have Right Relationships. As we will discuss later, this idea of stewardship is also key to our own conversion. As we become more and more aware of our role in this world as stewards of the earth and of the welfare of all creatures, we will begin to look at profits, the environment, business management, and many other issues in a very different light.

In our own time we have had opportunity to actually see a photograph of the earth from an astronaut's vehicle on the moon. I find looking at this photograph very meditative. I am first struck by how beautiful this "Blue Planet" is. I am next struck by how we really are one people. And I remain convinced that the things we use to differentiate and divide us (language, color, religion, political systems, etc.) can be overcome by these things that unite us: our common humanity, our universal ability to love truth and beauty, or desire to learn and appreciate this wonderful world around us, and our common identity as sons and daughters of God.

The Iroquois people in North America had what was called the seven-generation rule. Men and women were to use the goods of the earth in such a way as not to cause any harm for seven generations. Of course, if every generation was looking ahead seven generations, a very watchful stewardship would be going on.

The Year of Jubilees was perhaps more realistic in the sense of realizing that often it only takes about four generations to muddle things up, and by prescribing that at the end of that period there was to be a whole year concentrated on making things Right again.

## Teaching Regarding Justice and Distribution

In both cases there was a good amount of time spent reflecting on how people need to think of themselves as stewards of the earth. If we can really begin to think of ourselves as stewards—as joined, just people—and carry this out, we will have a peaceful society and world.

I am not talking about some sentimental, liberal, bleeding heart philosophy. The message is a radical one that has been the basis of law and human rights certainly in the West and in many Eastern countries as well. This message indeed gets to the heart or root of things. It is a message about conversion of the heart to justice. It is about making sure that all people within society are able to practice stewardship. A just society is of the utmost importance, and it takes change within people's hearts to achieve this.

This in no way minimizes its importance. What is at stake here is a set of values so basic to a healthy society that when it is not present societies collapse. This value of justice applies whether one believes in a God or not. When injustice is present it is like a disease; it tears societies apart. It is no respecter of people based on their belief or unbelief.

In our own time, one social critic who expressed many of the same concerns as the Old Testament prophets was musician and songwriter John Lennon of the Beatles. In his song "Imagine" he wrote:

> Imagine no possessions
> I wonder if you can
> No need for greed or hunger
> A brotherhood of man
> Imagine all the people—
> Sharing all the world . . .
>
> You may say I'm a dreamer
> But I'm not the only one
> I hope someday you'll join us
> And the world will be as one.[5]

---

5. John Lennon, "Imagine" (MacLean Music, 1971).

# 6

# New Testament Teachings Regarding Justice and Distribution

THE PURPOSE OF THIS chapter will be to examine what the New Testament has to say about our relationship to material wealth and the use of the world's goods. In this discussion we will not only deal with actual stories from the New Testament about material wealth and its distribution, we will also discuss some of the faith and theological conclusions of the early followers of Jesus.

Such an examination will want to include what Scripture scholars agree Jesus himself taught. But we also want to discuss broader New Testament teachings that discuss how we should use wealth and how we should share what we have.

Early church teachings about faith concerning Jesus runs through the Gospels, the New Testament letters, Acts, and Revelations. But since part of our goal is to present Jesus' own teachings about the distribution of wealth, we will look first at the Synoptic Gospels (Matthew, Mark, Luke). Although our discussion will begin with the Synoptic Gospels, we are not denigrating or dismissing the Gospel of John, Acts, or any of the letters. We will discuss them after our Synoptic presentation.

Scripture scholars have agreed for many decades that the search for the teachings of Jesus himself is a legitimate one, and that such a search bears its heaviest fruit through an examination of the Synoptic Gospels.

Certainly the Synoptic Gospels arose out of faith communities that had already come to an understanding of who Jesus was for them and what his life mission was about. But the Synoptic Gospels at times give us a view of Jesus' teachings and his life mission that seemed less interpretative and theological

# Teachings Regarding Justice and Distribution

than, say, the Gospel of John. There seems to be a clear attempt at times in the Synoptics to try to quote or approximate words of Jesus. There seems to be an attempt made to remember some of the parables he taught.

So looking at Jesus' teachings first through the Synoptic Gospels will be helpful in coming to an understanding of what Jesus taught about distribution of wealth. Such an approach will also help us understand more clearly why John, Paul, Peter, James, and Luke (in Acts) developed the faith and theological interpretation of Jesus they did.

As I read through the Synoptic Gospels to lift what most modern scholars agree are either the words of Jesus or teachings that probably reflect what he taught, it struck me how difficult it is to paraphrase or summarize what Jesus had to teach. The words of the Gospels are so simple and direct that they can, as the writer of Hebrews says, "slip through the place where the soul is divided from the spirit." More often than not, I let these words speak for themselves, letting the connotative and evocative language of the writer convey the message. Sometimes, though not often, I have been able to paraphrase one or the other parable. But as I have said, it is difficult to shorten or paraphrase what has already been said so well by the original writer. In addition, when one is trying to get to the essence of the Judeo-Christian teachings on any particular topic, it is best to let the sources speak for themselves.

## SYNOPTIC GOSPELS DISCUSSION

In Luke's Gospel, Jesus begins his peripatetic life of preaching about the Kingdom of God in the following manner:

> He came to Nazara, where he had been brought up, and went into the synagogue on the Sabbath day as he usually did. He stood up to read, and they handed him the scroll of the prophet Isaiah. Unrolling the scroll he found the place where it is written:
>
> The spirit of the lord has been given to me,
>
> For he has anointed me.
>
> He has sent me to bring the good news to the poor,
>
> To proclaim liberty to captives
>
> And to the blind new sight

A CONSCIOUS ENDEAVOR

>  To set the downtrodden free
>
>  To proclaim the Lord's year of favor.
>
>  He then rolled up the scroll, gave it back to the assistant and sat down. And all eyes in the synagogue were fixed on him. Then he began to speak to them, "This text is being fulfilled even as you listen." And he won the approval of all, and they were astonished at the gracious words that came from his lips. (Luke 4:16–22)

It is interesting that as Jesus begins his public life he immediately identifies himself with the "Lord's year of favor" as reported in the book of Isaiah. From the very beginning the writer of Luke's Gospel has Jesus identifying with the Year of Jubilees. Such a reference is made to emphasize that Jesus is thereby accepting the Old Testament ideal of distributive justice as represented in the Year of Jubilees, that jewel in the crown of Old Testament justice ideals.

Jesus would have known exactly what he was doing when he read from this text of Isaiah. He would have known what a powerful connotation the Year of Jubilees would have for his listeners. After all, Israel at the time was under Roman domination and ruled by foreign leaders with troops occupying all the major cities. One need only reflect on what it must have been like for the French, the Dutch, the Italians (occupied by the Germans), or the Chinese, the Filipinos, and the Koreans (occupied by the Japanese), or present-day Tibetans (occupied by the Chinese) to understand what Jews and Palestinians must have felt like in the time of Jesus. Luke mentions that those who heard him were "astonished at his gracious words." His words would certainly have been welcome during the time of Roman occupation and also by those who were being denied justice, particularly those who were poor.

Later in Luke's Gospel there is a parable that reflects Jesus' acceptance of another Old Testament theme about riches:

> Then he told them a parable: There was once a rich man who, having had a good harvest from his land thought to himself, "What am I to do? I have not enough room to store my crops." Then he said, "This is what I will do. I will pull down my barns and build bigger ones, and store all my grain and my goods in them, and I will say to my soul: Soul, you have plenty of good things laid by for many years to come; take things easy, eat, drink, and have a good time." But God said, "Fool! This very night the demand will be made for your soul; and this hoard of yours, whose will it be

## Teachings Regarding Justice and Distribution

> then?" So it is when a man stores up treasures for himself in place of making himself rich in the sight of God. (12:16–21)

Jesus repeats here an Old Testament theme: our lives are not to be defined by what we own. At the same time, he reiterates the idea that we should be living our lives in the face of death, with a healthy appreciation of our own mortality.

Not too long ago I was driving down the freeway when I was passed by someone with a very expensive car (I think it was a Mercedes or BMW). On the bumper of the car was a sticker that read, "He who dies with the most toys wins." This perspective is the antithesis of the scriptural perspective, which would see people who make consumerism and materialism the defining reality of their lives as losers. If we perceive our proper role as stewards instead of owners, then this temptation will not present itself with such force. Jesus ends the parable by telling his listeners they should make themselves rich in the sight of God. They will do this by entering into the secret place inside of themselves where conversion happens—where the Kingdom of God is.

There is a particularly beautiful and illustrative passage found in Matthew, Mark, and Luke that illustrates the idea of how we become rich in the sight of God.

> That is why I am telling you not to worry about your life and what you are to eat, not about your body and how you are to clothe it. Surely life means more than food, and the body more than clothing. Look at the birds of the sky. They do not sow or reap or gather into barns; yet your heavenly Father feeds them. Are you not worth much more than they are? Can any of you, for all his worrying, add one single cubit to his span of life? And why worry about clothing? Think of the Lilies of the fields; they never have to work or spin; yet I assure you that not even Solomon in all his regalia was robed like one of these. Now if that is how God clothes the grass in the field which is here today and thrown into the furnace tomorrow, will He not much more look after you, you men of little faith? So do not worry; do not say "What are we to eat? What are we to drink? How are we to be clothed?" It is the pagans who set their hearts on all these things. Your heavenly Father knows you need them all. Set your hearts on His kingdom first, and on His justice, and all these other things will be given to you as well. (Matt 6:25–34)

## A Conscious Endeavor

Jesus is not saying in this passage that we are not to toil and work. He is saying instead that we are not to work with our minds set first and foremost on what we will eat, drink, wear, or own. There are some people who are filled with pride for their possessions or avarice for the possessions of others. There are others who are so poor that they must always be thinking where their next meal will come from. Neither extreme is desirable. Rather, we are to toil and labor with our eyes first on the "Kingdom of God and his justice." Jesus is implying that if every person were concerned about justice first and foremost (a hallmark of the Kingdom), then everyone would have what they need.

To put it another way, Jesus is saying: God knows what you need. If you listen to the directives of God and honor them, you will have a society in which all men and women, as stewards, share the goods of the earth in such a manner that everyone's needs are taken care of.

The "Kingdom of God" is often on the lips of Jesus. This Kingdom is very near to us, it is inside of us. The Kingdom of God is what happens inside of people as they set themselves on the path of seeking God. As they come to understand who God is, their lives and relationships take on more loving, giving qualities. Their inner selves become more profoundly aware of why they are here and what their goal is in life. So it is with those who are seeking the Kingdom of God. Slowly, day by day, their lives will more perfectly mirror the love of God. As the writer of Hebrews says:

> The word of God is something alive and active: it cuts like a two-edged sword but more finely; it can slip through the place where the soul is divided from the spirit, or joints from the marrow; it can judge the secret emotions and thoughts. No created thing can hide from Him; everything is uncovered and open to the eyes of the one to whom we must give an account of ourselves. (4:12–13)

The person actively involved in conversion is aware of this secret place inside of them and spends a good deal of time there.

Another quality of soul that will flow out of us as we live the Kingdom of God in our relationships is justice. This idea of justice is colored differently by Jesus:

> He sat down opposite the treasury and watched the people putting money into the treasury, and many of the rich put in a great deal. A poor widow came and put in two small coins, the equivalent of a penny. Then he called his disciples and said to them, "I tell you solemnly, this poor widow has put more in than all who have

## Teachings Regarding Justice and Distribution

contributed to the treasury; for they have put in money they had over, but she from the little she had has put in everything she possessed, all she had to live on." (Mark 12:41–44)

We often talk these days about charity, philanthropy, and magnanimity. Usually what we mean by these ideas is donating either material goods or money we do not need to some organization or individual who is in need.

The scriptural approach would not look at things this way. Insofar as we think of our charity as something we might or might not do, that it is totally dependent on the goodness of our hearts, we have missed the point. In the Kingdom of God, sharing our goods with those who are in need is an obligation of justice. The popular notion of charity does not exist in the Scriptures. It is justice that binds us together. Doing acts of justice is the scriptural virtue.

There is another interesting story about those who live in the midst of riches. It is reported both in Matthew and Mark:

> He was setting out on a journey when a man ran up, knelt before him and put this question to him, "Good master, what must I do to gain eternal life?" Jesus said to him, "Why do you call me good? No one is good but God alone. You know the commandments: You must not kill; You must not commit adultery; You must not steal; You must not bring false witness; You must not defraud; Honor your father and mother." And he said to him, "I have kept all these from my earliest days." Jesus looked steadily at him and loved him, and he said, "There is one thing you lack. Go and sell everything you own and give the money to the poor, and you will have treasure in heaven; then come, follow me." But his face fell at these words and he went away sad, for he was a man of great wealth." (Mark 10:17–22)

This story is presented here very likely because it has a message beyond the particular rich man to whom Jesus was addressing himself.

Jesus is not suggesting in this story that everyone who is rich go and sell what they have and give the proceeds to the poor. This direction is given to one particular person.

Remember earlier when we discussed how revelation will always have a radical message, something that gets right to the root of things? Here we have a case of a particular young man who is very wealthy and is striving to live a good life.

## A Conscious Endeavor

He wants to know what more he can do. Jesus in an apparently loving manner points out to this man that he is too attached to his wealth. The best thing he can do is get rid of it.

Not all people can live in the midst of great wealth and not be ruined by it. Some can, and some cannot. This particular young man could not. Certainly it is easy for us to understand that with wealth comes power. Many are drugged by the power wealth brings.

At the same time, there are some men and women who can live in the midst of great wealth and it seems to mean nothing to them in the sense it does not become an obsession. Such people usually see their mortality and their role as stewards.

When I was building affordable housing in San Jose, California, I had the occasion to meet David Packard a couple of times. We were both attending a business conference. I was struck by his humility. While this man was one of the Silicon Valley giants, a man whose counsel presidents sought, it struck me that he was almost surprised he had become wealthy. He was very down to earth, and certainly knew the social responsibilities of those who control wealth. He went about doing his stewardship quietly, behind the scenes. He was a modest man. Men such as he do exist in the community of wealth, but sadly they seem all too few.

In Luke we have the story about another man of wealth, Zacchaeus:

> He entered Jericho and was going through the town when a man whose name was Zacchaeus made his appearance; he was one of the senior tax collectors and a wealthy man. He was anxious to see what kind of a man Jesus was, but he was too short and could not see him for the crowd; so he ran up ahead and climbed a sycamore tree to catch a glimpse of Jesus who was to pass that way. When Jesus reached the spot he looked up and spoke to him: "Zacchaeus, come down. Hurry, because I must stay at your house today." And he hurried down and welcomed him joyfully. They all complained when they saw what was happening. "He has gone to stay at a sinner's house" they said. But Zacchaeus—stood his ground and said to Jesus, "Look, sir, I am going to give half my property to the poor, and if I have cheated anybody I will pay him back four times the amount." And Jesus said, "Today salvation has come to this house, because this man too is a son of Abraham; for the Son of Man has come to seek out and save what was lost. (19:1–10)

## Teachings Regarding Justice and Distribution

Zacchaeus was the type of man his peers loved to hate. He collected taxes for the Roman government. He was seen as a traitor to his own people. And he became quite wealthy in the doing, making him even more despicable.

Certainly Zacchaeus was in a position to throw his weight around, overtaxing people, and he apparently did this. But as he was a man seeking to do good, after conversing at length with Jesus about things on his mind, he came to some decisions. The main decision he made was to be more just in his relationships. This meant correcting many errors he had made with people whom he had overcharged, and also sharing his wealth with those in need. He became aware of his role as a steward, and at the same time apparently made some decisions about honesty in business as well.

Jesus states that "today salvation [healing] has come to this house." Not only is life going to be different for Zacchaeus, but for all who live in his household. A change brought about inside Zacchaeus affects all those around him.

The last three of our discussions about wealth in the teachings of Jesus are in three parables: the parable of the crafty steward, the parable of the talents (pounds), and the parable of the workers in the vineyard.

All three of these parables are strange both in the telling and in the conclusions one might draw from them.

> There was a rich man and he had a steward who was denounced to him for being wasteful with his property. He called for the man and said, "What is this I hear about you? Draw me up an account of your stewardship because you are not to be my steward any longer." Then the steward said to himself, "Now that my master is taking the stewardship from me, what am I to do? Dig? I am not strong enough. Go begging? I should be too ashamed. Ah, I know what I will do to make sure that when I am dismissed from office there will be some to welcome me into their homes. Then he called his master's debtors one by one. To the first he said, "How much do you owe my master?" "One hundred measures of oil" was the reply. The steward said, "Here, take your bond; sit down straight away and write fifty." To another he said, "And you, sir, how much do you owe?" One hundred measures of wheat" was the reply. The steward said, "Here, take your bond and write eighty." The master praised the dishonest steward for his astuteness. For the children of this world are more astute in dealing with their own kind than are the children of light. And so I tell you this: use money, tainted as it is, to win you friends, and thus make sure that when it fails you, they will welcome you into the tents of eternity. (Luke 16:1–9)

Stewards in households of this time were usually born into the household. They had great discretion in how they handled their master's accounts. It was not unknown for stewards to add on extra to these accounts to make some money for themselves. It is likely that this steward indulged in these practices. When he squared the accounts, he probably reduced the notes without the extra he was charging for his own accounts.

There seem to be two messages in this parable. One is that the crafty steward certainly knew how to square accounts in such a way as to make himself well liked by the debtors, which would stand him well in the future. By introducing some honesty at this point, he is manifesting a certain prudence and craftiness in working with wealth.

I am most intrigued by the second message of the parable: "use money as tainted as it is, to win friends . . ." I don't think Jesus is talking about buying friendship, as in political buyoffs, for instance.

Friendships are horizontal relationships, as opposed to vertical relationships. Wealth tends to create vertical relationships: exaggerated differences between the haves and the have-nots; the powerful exercising their power over those who have less.

Jesus seems to be saying that when wealth is used correctly it creates horizontal relationships. This does not mean that all people will have the same amount of wealth. However, there can be horizontal relationships between those who have more and those who have less, because all are stewards. Therefore people can form friendships.

To some extent, this gets at the problem of class. We have seen the different classes that are created by having or not having wealth. Certain classes never mix. Wealthier people look down on poorer people. There is always someone to look down upon.

Class distinctions—placing value on human beings based on their wealth—goes against the grain of what is being said in this parable. When our wealth becomes a reason for us to think we are better than someone else because of it, then our wealth is destroying our humanity. We would be better off to do what Jesus counsels the rich young man to do: get rid of it, for it certainly is not a source of positive growth for us.

Ideally, there is a way for people who have more and people who have less to rub elbows and form friendships. This should be able to happen. When we create societies that discourage this, whether in terms of neighborhoods, businesses, or other institutions, we are not using wealth the way it was intended.

## Teachings Regarding Justice and Distribution

The parable of the talents (pounds) is found in Matthew and Luke in full form, and in a shortened form in Mark as well:

> [The Kingdom of Heaven/God] is like a man on his way abroad who summoned his servants and entrusted his property to them. To one he gave five talents, to another two, to a third one; each in proportion to his ability. Then he set out. The man who had received the five talents promptly went and traded with them and made five more. The man who had received two made two more in the same way. But the man who had received one went off and dug a hole in the ground and hid his master's money. Now a long time after, the master of those servants came back and went through his accounts with them. The man who had received the five talents came forward with five more," "Sir," he said, "You entrusted me with five talents; here are five more that I have made." His master said to him, "Well done good and faithful servant; you have shown you can be faithful in small things, I will trust you with greater; come and join in your master's happiness." Next the man with the two talents came forward. "Sir," he said, "You entrusted me with two talents; here are two more that I have made." His master said to him, "Well, done, good and faithful servant; you have shown you can be faithful in small things, I will entrust you with greater; come and join in your master's happiness." Last came forward the man who had the one talent. "Sir," he said, "I had heard you were a hard man, reaping where you have not sown and gathering where you have not scattered; so I was afraid, and I went off and hid your talent in the ground. Here it is; it was yours, you have it back." But his master answered him, "You wicked and lazy servant! So you knew that I reap where I have not sown and gather where I have not scattered? Well then, you should have deposited my money with the bankers, and on my return I would have recovered my capital with interest. So now take the talent from him and give it to the man who has the five talents. For to everyone who has will be given more, and he will have more than enough; but from the man who has not, even that will be taken away. As for this good-for-nothing servant, throw him out into the dark, where there will be weeping and grinding of teeth. (Matt 25:14–30)

This parable is interesting in the fact that Jesus used an example of how we handle material wealth and employment as a fit way to describe what the Kingdom of God is like.

The sums of money are considerable. Five talents was about thirty thousand pieces of silver. So we are talking about a person leaving a lot of wealth in his servants' keeping.

There were metaphorical and perhaps even allegorical meanings in this parable for the early Christians. For example, when one is given the gift of faith but does not share it, one can expect some divine retribution. To put such allegorical interpretations in our own time and language, we could ask, what if Mozart had not written any music? What would his accounting with God be like?

But since Jesus seemed to find it appropriate to use this story to talk about the Kingdom of God, then the level at which he talks about wealth must be likewise appropriate. This is one of the few stories he ever told about the responsibilities between employers and employees (the vineyard workers being the only other that comes to mind).

At the beginning of the story, the master (boss, owner, employer) gives responsibilities according to the actual abilities of his employees. He doesn't place less or more responsibility on them than they can handle. This does not seem to be a whimsical reporting on Jesus' part, but an acknowledgment by Jesus that the master in this example of stewardship has the obligation to recognize peoples' abilities and put them to their best use.

The story states clearly that the servants (employees) have an obligation to the master (employer) to work hard and to the best of their ability. When they do so they not only create wealth for their employer, but wealth for themselves as well. In applying him/herself assiduously, the employee learns more, develops his/her skills, and in the long run enhances his/her abilities to create sufficient wealth, to where he/she will eventually have even more than enough, if we are to believe this story.

On the other hand, the person who does not work in a manner consistent with his/her abilities will very likely be turned loose.

Obviously, the employer/employee relationship is a complex one. However, the story is insightful for getting at the root of this relationship. The employer in the story respects the creativity of the individual employee. And in this particular story, most of the employees respond to this respect and trust by increasing substantially the wealth of their employer.

In response, the employer in the story invites such employees into greater intimacy with him. It seems clear as well that as the employee creates wealth, the employer shares part of that wealth with the employee.

# Teachings Regarding Justice and Distribution

We will be referring back to this story when we discuss employer/employee relationships, unions, profit sharing, and other issues arising in our day.

The parable of the workers in the vineyard is one that has caused as much consternation to readers today as the workers in the parable itself:

> Now the kingdom of heaven is like a landowner going out at daybreak to hire workers for his vineyard. He made an agreement with the workers for one denarius (a day's wage) a day, and sent them into his vineyard. Going out at about the third hour he saw others standing idle in the market place and said to them, "You go to my vineyard too and I will give you a fair wage." So they went. At about the sixth hour and again at about the ninth hour, he went out and did the same. Then at about the eleventh hour he went out and found more men standing round, and he said to them, "Why have you been standing here idle all day?" "Because no one has hired us," they answered. He said to them, "You go into my vineyard too. In the evening, the owner said to his bailiff, "Call the workers and pay them their wages, starting with the last arrivals and ending with the first." So those who were hired at about the eleventh hour came forward and received one denarius each. When the first came, they expected to get more, but they too received one denarius each. They took it, but grumbled at the landowner. "The men who came last," they said, "have done only one hour, and you have treated them the same as us, though we have done a heavy day's work in all the heat." He answered one of them and said, "My friend, I am not being unjust to you; did we not agree on one denarius? Take your earnings and go. I choose to pay the last-comer as much as I pay you. Have I no right to do what I like with my own? Why be envious because I am generous. Thus the last will be first and the first last." (Matt 20:1–16)

This is another parable that has been rich in allegorical meaning for early Christians. But again, we will look at it only in relation to the use of work in describing what the Kingdom of God is like.

It seems here we have the situation of many people doing the same work, but some for a shorter period during the same day.

This going out to the marketplace to find laborers is as common in our urban areas today as it was back in the time of Jesus.

The employer in the story is interested in paying a fair or just wage. Apparently the denarius was thought to be a just wage for one day's work. An important aspect of the wage being a just wage is the acceptance of this fact by the worker. The employer says, "Come to work and I will pay you a fair wage, namely, X." The worker says, "I accept that as a just wage."

In every case in which the employer goes out seeking employees, such a conversation takes place. It is therefore safe to say that, in Jesus' mind, the reporting of it is important. In every case, a discussion of a just wage takes place and then people go to work.

At the end of the day, of course, those who had worked for only one hour get paid the amount considered a just wage for a whole day's work, just like the others. This causes grumbling among those who had worked all day.

If one keeps in mind that this is casual labor, we realize that the employer knows this is the only money all the workers will get that day, and that even though some have not been hired till later, their families' needs are the same. Perhaps, as he is trying to be a just man, he knows that if he pays all of them what is considered a just day's wage, they will all be able to procure for their families what they need.

It is just as likely that if the same people who worked only an hour are hired tomorrow at the beginning of the day and get paid a day's wage, they will be the ones grumbling.

In an imperfect world, the employer who is trying to be a good steward, like the employer in the parable, will try to pay a just wage. We will discuss minimum wage later and try to have an intelligent discussion about whether what is considered minimum wage is a just wage, and whether or not it should be.

The important point is that the employer and employee have a discussion over the fairness (justice) of wages.

The parable seems to conclude that, assuming this discussion has taken place and there is agreement between two parties, then anything paid above and beyond a fare wage to particular individuals is a matter between the employer and those employees.

The same type of grumbling also occurs over employment not of the casual labor type. For instance, Joe has been on the job for fifteen years. Mary is hired to do the same work, and starts at the same pay that Joe receives. Many of the Joes in the world will not think this fair. What they need to ask is, "Am I getting a just wage?" If they are, then they have to trust that the employer has evaluated Mary relative to her abilities and background. In other words, he might have very good reasons for paying Mary the same amount as Joe.

Teachings Regarding Justice and Distribution

## ST. JOHN: GOSPEL AND LETTERS

After leaving the Synoptic Gospels, which in many ways seem like "a day in the life" of Jesus, we turn to the Gospel of John. John's Gospel is a very deep and rich reflection on the incredible love God has for us.

From the prologue, ("In the beginning was the Word . . .") John's Gospel echoes in some ways the book of Genesis. Just as in Genesis creation takes place in the midst of a dark and confused void, so for John the Word of God (Jesus) brings light to a darkened world. The theme of darkness and light will arise over and over again in John. For him, Jesus is, among other things, the enlightened one. Jesus is the one who comes from the world of light and brings enlightenment to us.

John often contrasts darkness and light in his stories. Consider the story of the woman at the well in Samaria (John 4). Jesus meets the woman at the well, and asks her for a drink. She is surprised that a Jew would even talk to a Samaritan, and a woman at that. Jesus responds that if she knew what God was offering her, she would ask him for a drink. She notices that he has no bucket. She is not "getting" what Jesus is talking about. She is interpreting things on an unenlightened level. With regard to the truth Jesus is presenting, she (being a symbol of all of us) is in darkness. Jesus then speaks to her of living water. She mentions that she would like some of this living water. Jesus tells her go and get her husband and come back. At this point, the woman has to examine her life and realizes she has had a problem with relationships. "I have no husband," she says, and then hurriedly changes the subject. The subject of her husbands is obviously painful to her. She now wants to talk about where Jews and Samaritans worship, and their hope for a Messiah. Jesus says that the person they are looking for is before her now. Finally, she understands what Jesus has been trying to communicate, as if scales had been removed from her eyes. And so it goes with many of the stories in John's Gospel. People are led from darkness to light.

John often portrays in his Gospel that in order to understand what Jesus is talking about you need to look at things from a whole new point of view.

The story of Nicodemus states this theme eloquently. Nicodemus is a Pharisee. He is drawn to Jesus, but because of his position in the community he is afraid to be seen with Jesus in the light of day. This unenlightened but good man must come to see Jesus at night! Jesus tells him how he must be born again from above. Nicodemus interprets this only on the unenlightened level, and wonders how he can crawl back in his mother's womb to be reborn. I can imagine Jesus smiling and saying lightheartedly, "Oy vey! Nicodemus, you're just not getting it. Let's go over this again!" So Jesus starts again, and explains to Nicodemus how the person "who lives by the truth, comes out into the light, so that it may be plainly seen that what he does is done in God" (John 3:21). Then, finally, Nicodemus gets it.

John sees Jesus as the one who came from above, from the Father, and who is going back to the Father. But before going back to the Father, Jesus will share with us the incredible gift of God's love, and enlighten us on what it means to live a life in the Spirit.

John's Gospel develops a profound reflection on the richness and depth that Jesus, the Word of God, both reveals to us and shares with us. One of the obvious conclusions the Gospel wants us to draw is that if God shares so generously his riches with us, then we too should share with one another.

There is an interesting point John makes in his story of the first miracle at the wedding in Cana (John 2:1–12). We are all familiar with the story. Jesus is at a wedding. Wedding feasts often went on for days in Jesus' time. Since people traveled long distances by camel, donkey, or on foot, a wedding feast was not just an afternoon affair. People came together who had not seen each other for probably quite some time. They spent a few days renewing friendships and celebrating the goodness of their lives within the context of the wedding feast.

Jesus's mother, Mary, comes to him when they had run out of wine at the feast and tells him the wine is gone. Jesus asks, "Why do you turn to me? My hour has not yet come." We know that in this story Jesus did respond, and the wine was replenished. What is interesting to me is that even though Jesus does not think it is time for him to respond, in fact, does not want to respond, he does.

Later, when Jesus is arrested and Peter strikes off the ear of the guard of the high priest, Jesus, after healing the ear, says, "Am I not to drink from the cup the Father has given me?"

Jesus seems to understand very early on in his ministry that it is when we are called upon to do something we do not want to do, and at a time in our lives when we think the timing is all wrong (perhaps we do not think we have the talent, the time, or adequate preparation), but we rise to the challenge anyway, then miracles happen.

We can apply this message to our handling of situations in life where the wealth of the world is not being distributed justly. There are many situations that might call themselves to our attention regarding justice and the distribution of wealth. We might not want to become involved in the

## Teachings Regarding Justice and Distribution

solutions to these problems. We might not think we are ready. But if we rise to the challenge and become involved, much can be accomplished.

It is often only when we are challenged to go beyond what we thought were our limits that we discover the deep resources of strength, love, and compassion in our souls. "A man's reach should exceed his grasp, or else, what's heaven for?"

John's Gospel exhorts us over and over again to "walk as children of the light.... Anyone who claims to be in the light, but hates his brother, is still in the dark." (1 John 2:9). He says our love is not to be just talk, but something real and active (1 John 3:18). John defines the relationship between love and fear: "In love there can be no fear. But fear is driven out by perfect love: because to fear is to expect punishment; and anyone who is still afraid is imperfect in love" (1 John 4:17).

Much of our economic theory and the ways we distribute wealth is fear based. Our unwillingness to share what we have, John would probably say, is based on a fear that if we do share there will not be enough for us, or perhaps that people will take advantage of us. John is very clear: love involves trust, generosity, and thankfulness. "Look at the love the Father has lavished on us by letting us be called God's children; and that is what we are!" (1 John 3:1). "If a man who was rich enough in this world's goods saw that one of his brothers was in need, and closed his heart to him, how could the love of God be living in him?" (1 John 3:17). John is famous for asking the question: How can a man say he loves the God he cannot see, if he does not love the brother he can see? (1 John 4:20).

John's spirituality is very simple and very practical. When you see a need, respond out of the love of God. You will know that you love God if you love those around you, especially those in need.

## ST. PAUL

Paul's letters are rich in exhortations to "make real friends with the poor" (Rom 12:16). Paul makes himself very clear: "... if we live, we live for the Lord, and if we die, we die for the Lord so that alive or dead we belong to the Lord" (Rom 14:7–8). Paul continually reminds us that everything belongs to God, including ourselves: You are Christ's, and Christ is God's (1 Cor 3:23). Paul calls to mind the Old Testament theme that God is the creator who has given us the earth as a place to work out our stewardship.

## A Conscious Endeavor

Paul's view is very similar to John's. Just as John sees our lives as a response to the generous love of God, so, too, does Paul. Paul exhorts us again and again to be generous with our lives and possessions. Why? Because God has loved us first. "He chose us, chose us in Christ, to be holy and spotless, and to live through love in his presence, determining that we should become his adopted sons . . . his free gift to us in the Beloved, . . . Such is the richness of the grace which he has showered on us in all wisdom and insight." (Eph 1:6–11).

Paul wants to rid us of our self-righteousness before God. It is common to meet people who think they have earned everything they have in life, especially their earthly possessions. When a person emphasizes too greatly his/her self-reliance and achievements, this can become misguided pride. In St. Paul's letters he takes a very different approach. He reminds us: God did everything first. He created. He gave us the Christ. He has sent us his Spirit. Everything is a gift. Life itself is a gift. Our response is to live a life of thankfulness and generosity. "What do you have that was not given to you? And if it was given, how can you boast as though it were not?"[1] Our lives are not about self-righteousness and making demands because we have "earned" this or that. Our lives are to be a realization that everything is a gift, and our response is to be one of gratefulness to God and generously sharing of everything we have, even our very selves.

Just as for Paul Jesus did not deem his equality with God something to be clung to, but emptied himself and took the form of a servant (Phil 2), so we are to do the same thing, *because Christ did it first*!

Paul's great hymn to love (1 Cor 13:1–13) warns us that no matter what we do, if it is not done out of love, we are falling short of the mark. For Paul, all the gifts we possess, even our very lives, are to serve God's purposes. There is no other reason for our existence. In 2 Corinthians he states, "we are only the earthenware jars that hold this treasure [our souls, or very being], to make it clear that such an overwhelming power comes from God, and not from us" (4:7). In Ephesians he prays, "Out of his infinite glory, may he give you the power through his Spirit for your hidden self to grow strong, so that Christ may live in your hearts through faith, and then, planted in love and built on love, you will with all the saints have strength to grasp the breadth and the length, the height and the depth; until, knowing the love of Christ, which is beyond all knowledge, you are filled with the utter fullness of God." (3:16–19). For Paul, everything is about making our hidden self grow strong,

---

1. 1 Cor 4:7.

## Teachings Regarding Justice and Distribution

so that we can be planted in and built on love. Paul's concern is similar to that of Jesus when he teaches us about prayer. Jesus talks about entering into that secret place (what Paul calls our hidden self) where the Father, who knows what is going on in that secret place, will reward us.

Paul is clear about the riches we should be paying attention to: our inner spirit and the Spirit of God. Our purpose here is to recognize and give assent to the generosity of God, and to live a life in the Spirit, giving thanks and being generous. For Paul, since one man died for many, we should no longer live for ourselves (2 Cor 5:15). "Remember how generous the Lord Jesus was: he was rich, but he became poor for your sake, to make you rich out of his poverty" (2 Cor 8:9).

Central to Paul's preaching is the idea of "putting on the new self." "Your mind must be renewed by a spiritual revolution" (Eph 4:23). Paul speaks constantly about the conversion process we discussed earlier as being at the heart of his message.

Paul's conclusions about wealth resound with Old Testament themes and the idea of stewardship: "Warn those who are rich in this world's goods that they are not to look down on other people; and not to set their hopes on money, which is untrustworthy, but on God who, out of his riches, gives us all that we need for our happiness. Tell them that they are to do good, and be rich in good works, to be generous, and willing to share—this is the way they can save up a good capital sum for the future if they want to make sure of the only life that is real." (1 Tim 6:17–19). This conversation is reminiscent of the story from Luke mentioned earlier about hoarding riches. Jesus admonished his listeners in this story about a man who built bigger barns for his riches, but then died: "So it is when a man stores up treasure for himself in place of making himself rich in the sight of God." (Luke 12:21).

## JAMES

The letter of James is steeped in the Jewish traditions out of which he came. James reflects the Old Testament moral obligation to look after for the poor. "... do not," he says, "try to combine faith in Jesus Christ ... with the making of distinctions between classes of people." (2:2). He even goes so far as to say that as soon as you make distinctions between classes of people based on wealth, you are committing sin (2:5–10).

When James discusses faith and works, he says, "Do realize, you senseless man, that faith without good deeds is useless?" He concludes "A body dies when it is separated from the spirit, and in the same way faith is dead if it is separated from good deeds."[2] James concludes his letter with a reminder that is reminiscent of the Old Testament's and Jesus' reminders of how we should live our lives with our death before our eyes. His words are strong: "Here is the answer for those of you who talk like this: 'Today or tomorrow, we are off to this or that town; we are going to spend a year there, trading, and making money.' You never know what will happen tomorrow: you are no more than a mist that is here for a little while and then disappears. The most you should ever say is this: 'If it is the Lord's will, we shall be alive to do this or that.' (4:13–15). "Now an answer for the rich. Start crying, weep for the miseries that are coming to you. Your wealth is all rotting . . . All your gold and silver are corroding away. . . . Labourers mowed your fields and you cheated them—listen to the wages you kept back, calling out; realize that the cries of the reapers have reached the ears of the Lord of Hosts" (5:1–4). James is clear in calling us to our obligations to others under the Old Testament concept of justice.

## ACTS OF THE APOSTLES

In the book of Acts there is a wonderful description of the communal ownership of some of the early Christian communities (2:44–47). Some Christians saw a tribal or cooperative lifestyle as one valid way to share the goods of the earth. This theme has been constant in Christianity through the centuries, and is still practiced today in monasteries, convents, and other religious communes throughout the world. This same lifestyle is described a second time in Acts 4:32–35: "The whole group of believers was united, heart and soul; no one claimed for his own use anything that he had, as everything they owned was held in common. The apostles continued to testify to the resurrection of the Lord Jesus with great power, and they were all given great respect. None of their members was ever in want, as all those who owned land or houses would sell them, and bring the money from them, to present it to the apostles; it was then distributed to any members who might be in need."

What strikes the reader when reading Acts of the Apostles is the extreme material generosity of the early followers of Jesus.

As in the Old Testament, care for widows and orphans is used as a measuring rod as to whether the early Christian communities were living

---

2. Jas 2:20, 26.

an authentic life in light of the teachings (see Acts 6:1–6). In other words, the widow and orphan continued to be symbols of society's weakest members. The early Christian communities were considered to be falling short of the ideal if they were not paying attention to the needs of their most needy members.

In the documentation of Paul's travels in Acts, we have an interesting account of how the preaching in Ephesus caused some alarm amongst the silversmiths (19:23–41). It seems the silversmith's guild in Ephesus thought that the successful establishment of Christianity in Ephesus would endanger their revenues as manufacturers of statues of the goddess Diana. One can draw conclusions that the message of Jesus might often negatively affect certain peoples' profits. The point here is that often a person who is involved in the process of conversion will legitimately make a choice to not buy certain products or patronize certain establishments and businesses because of their unethical business or political practices.

One can think in our own time of the successful use of economic sanctions against South Africa in order to get them to end Apartheid. It can often be a uniquely Christian approach to challenge evil by taking the profit out of it. Boycotts have been one of the most successful ways of doing this. Boycotts are non-violent, but they say very clearly, "We are going to show you that, even in a worldly sense, evil and injustice are not profitable."

Perhaps the most poetic description of the early generosity of the Christian communities is expressed by Peter (Acts 3:6) in his cure of the lame man. Peter says, "I will have neither silver nor gold, but I will give you what I have: in the name of Jesus Christ the Nazarene, walk!" One senses a readiness to share whatever one has, whether materially or in the Spirit, in these early Christians as described by the wonderful book of Acts.

## CONCLUSION

Our discussion of the distribution of wealth in the New Testament has been brief. But it is clear what our attitude should be. Any discussion of money and power as discussed in the Gospels and letters can only end in the same place Jesus ended the discussion in his own life. Towards the end of his life, when he was with his disciples and he knew his death was imminent, he gathered them together for a very intimate Passover meal.

## A Conscious Endeavor

There among a group of men and women who looked up to him as the greatest teacher they had ever known, the following is reported to have occurred:

> They were at supper ... and he got up from table, removed his outer garment and, taking a towel, wrapped it round his waist; he then poured water into a basin and began to wash the disciples' feet and to wipe them with the towel he was wearing.... When he had washed their feet and put on his clothes again he went back to the table. "Do you understand," he said "what I have done to you? You call me Master and Lord, and rightly; so I am. If I, then, the Lord and Master, have washed your feet, you should wash each other's feet. I have given you an example so that you may copy what I have done to you. (John 13:2–16)

This, of course, is reminiscent of what he had said in Matthew:

> You know that among the pagans the rulers lord it over them, and their great men make their authority felt. This is not to happen among you. No; anyone who wants to be great among you must be your servant, ... (Matt 20:25–27)

# 7
# Defining the Task

THE TASK OF ANY man or woman who is trying to walk the path of the Judeo-Christian value system in today's world is difficult but achievable. The perspective he/she brings is not one of presenting to people a political system or an economic system that measures up to the message inherent in the spiritual perspective. We are not talking here about putting together a political party, government, or economic system that could be branded as Jewish or Christian. This has certainly been tried, and there even exist today such political parties in the United States (the religious right), Italy (the Christian Socialist Party), and in other countries. But I do not think this is the direction that true spiritual conversion will take.

Religious faith tries to deal with what it considers to be the most important aspect of men and women, namely, their spiritual life. The process of conversion that we discussed earlier in chapters 2 and 3 is a matter of the inner growth of the human spirit.

Saying the spiritual development of the inner person is the most important aspect of who we are and why we are here does not mean that the other parts of our lives are unimportant. Obviously food, clothing, shelter, education, and our work are important. But, "... life means more than food, and the body more than clothing" (Luke 12:23). All these other things are peripheral to nourishing the inner spirit. It is in the midst of all these other realities of our lives that our spirit discovers who and what it is. The person who is taking his/her conversion seriously is aware of the importance of the growth of the spirit.

Let us go back to our discussion of the vase in the middle of the room. As we said earlier, as we walk around the room, we will get a different perspective of the vase. Each perspective is different, but has its own validity. As you will recall, we began naming these perspectives: philosophy, science, poetry, music, economics, etc.

We said that the vase represented our life, and that life has many perspectives. We said that each perspective helps us understand our life in a different way.

Let us now add something new to our metaphor of the vase. Let us say that there is a huge 100,000 carat uncut diamond inside the vase. Let us say this diamond is our spirit. Just as the diamond is uncut and needs to be formed and polished to become a beautiful diamond, so the spirit needs to achieve growth. We call this growth conversion.

There are two things we can say about this diamond/spirit. Though the diamond is inside the vase, it is by far the most valuable. At the same time, as we walk around the vase (consider other perspectives) we might not see the diamond, but our various perspectives of the vase will be incomplete to the extent that they do not discover and acknowledge that the diamond is there.

Since the scientific revolution in which Copernicus and Galileo pointed out that the earth was not the center of the universe, there has developed an enmity between science and religion. Much of this may have resulted from the reaction of the religious community to the findings of science. Some scientists were burned at the stake, and others were excommunicated. Religion has often been very narrow-minded about scientific discovery. Both disciplines have therefore lacked the ability to blend their various perspectives into a unified approach to reality.

Science does and should have its independent methods of investigation. However, science needs to be as careful about materialistic reductionism as religion needs to be about intolerance. If any discipline limits perception of reality to a particular and limited perspective, that discipline will have a skewed viewpoint that is limiting rather than liberating.

When we say the human spirit is the most important, we mean that our soul or spirit is the center or our being, and, in many religious faiths, will be something that endures when the physical aspect of our humanity diminishes and disappears at death. It is the spirit that ultimately interprets and unifies all the other perspectives: science, music, art, economics, philosophy, etc. It is the soul in each of us that is being either nurtured or destroyed by what is occurring around and about us. I am reminded of one of the more poetic lines of Paul:

## Defining the Task

> We are only the earthenware jars that hold this treasure, to make it clear that such an overwhelming power comes from God, and not from us. (2 Cor 4:7)

As we mentioned above, the diamond is uncut, in the rough, as they say. Like the diamond, the soul must be shaped by the performance of its task of putting together its life in a way that creates beauty. As the prophet Jeremiah says:

> So I went down to the potter's house; and there he was, working at the wheel. And whenever the vessel he was making came out wrong, as happens with the clay handled by potters, he would start afresh and work it into another vessel, as potters do. Then this word of Yahweh was addressed to me: "House of Israel, can not I do to you what this potter does? . . . Yes, as the clay is in the potter's hand, so are you in Mine." (18:3–7)

As we perform the task of interrelating all the different perspectives of life into a unified whole that creates meaning, we need to keep in mind that most important of all our life tasks is shaping our soul. And this is our inner conversion.

The task before us in discussing our economic relationships will be initiated with this in mind. While our economic lives are the manner by which we provide for our material well-being, the whole purpose of our economics will miss the mark if it does not pay attention to the inner spirit. Our economic systems should be as concerned with developing things that feed and clothe the soul as they are with feeding and clothing the body.

As we discuss the economic perspective, it will be necessary as well to discuss the political perspective since the two are so interwoven. But as we do so, we need to keep the following thought in mind: the importance of these perspectives and the "truth" they might speak about reality have value only insofar as they lead to the growth of the human spirit.

The question has been asked: Is there a Judeo-Christian political or economic system? The short answer is no. There never has been, nor will there ever be, despite the best efforts of the State of Israel, Charlemagne's Holy Roman Empire, Spain under Ferdinand and Isabel as well as Philip II, or England under Henry VIII. All of these governments represent political/economic systems subject to a particular religious perspective. Each of them has been uniquely arrogant toward and intolerant of any other perspective, often committing murder in the name of religion. We can see this today, as we have seen it for years, in the Middle East (centuries of internecine murder in the name of religion) and in Northern Ireland, to name but two troubled areas of our globe that have their roots in religious differences. One can call this nothing but what it is: a horrific and shameful scandal.

The ideal presented to us in the Scriptures has never been to establish an external "Kingdom of God." As Jesus said, the Kingdom of God is inside you. When we begin to think of establishing some type of political, economic, and religious government or institution we are already in the world of Professor Harold Hill and religious hucksterism.

The role that women and men of the Judeo-Christian stamp are meant to play is akin to that of the prophet. As we saw earlier, the prophet played the role of the radical messenger who proclaimed a message that cut right to the root of problems within his/her society, especially regarding the treatment of those who were disenfranchised, poor, or treated unjustly. The prophet knew that how the weaker members of the society were treated served as a barometer of the overall health of society.

The prophet played the role of calling people back to Right Relationships with God, each other, and the earth. The prophet was primarily concerned with the inner human spirit, and what the actions of men and women in society were doing to their spirits. The prophet was interested in the conversion of those around him/her as well as him/herself.

One contemporary example of people who have played a prophetic role is the founders of Ben and Jerry's Ice Cream. In a world of business often destructive of the environment in its production methods, and destructive of the human spirit in its management, these two men served as a successful and prophetic enigma in today's business world. They bought only natural products for their ice cream. They made sure the dairies that supplied them did not use bovine growth hormone. They also made sure the farmers who raised the herds of cows did not use dangerous chemicals in the feed given to the cows. From start to finish, their ice cream was environmentally safe. The company even spent a share of its profits to help buy public lands in South America to preserve tropical rain forests.

In terms of internal management, a team approach was fostered. There was a profit-sharing plan for employees. There was a tendency to promote from inside the company rather than hire from without.

The company was financially successful, and served as an example of how a business can be humanly and environmentally accountable and still make a handsome profit. The company was able to operate within the context of competitive capitalism, but created a new moral environment

## Defining the Task

within that context. It was a company involved in the process of conversion, affecting the quality of the day in a competitive capitalist market. On April 24, 2001, while I was driving home from work, I happened to catch a story about Ben and Jerry's Ice Cream being sold to a larger corporation. The first practices to go: using only milk products that do not use bovine growth hormones and other harmful chemicals, and the socially conscious investment of a portion of profits in preserving rain forests in South America. Profit is all that matters to some corporations.

At the opposite end of the spectrum is Dorothy Day. Day was the founder of the Catholic Worker Movement in the United States. Ms. Day went through a period of atheism in the 1920s. In the 1930s, during the Great Depression, she converted to Catholicism and began feeding the poor in Hell's Kitchen of New York. She was known for establishing a soup kitchen in the Bowry and operating houses of hospitality for those who had no place to live but the streets. She became a social critic. She focused on economic policies, immigration laws, discrimination (racial prejudice), war (especially nuclear arms), and the rights of workers to organize unions for social justice. What she began in Hell's Kitchen became an influential voice calling the Catholic community and others to conversion. At the same time, she joined with others who wanted to work towards a society that had more respect for the rights of all human beings and the nurturing of the human spirit. She died in 1980.

Dorothy Day thought she should be a burr under the saddle of people in positions of power who could effect just distribution of wealth, calling them to conversion.

Ben and Jerry and Dorothy Day lived out their lives the way they thought they heard their inner voice telling them to live. You will live your life out according to your own inner calling. Everyone is unique, and each of us must find his/her own path and way of life. But one thing we can say of those trying to live out the Judeo-Christian traditions is that they are meant to live a life that gives voice to a deeper muse.

The men and women of today who are coming to their businesses from a Judeo-Christian background will listen to this muse and apply it in their own business relationships. Their conversion process will allow them to take a reflective step back from the economic system in which they find themselves. This stepping back will allow them to analyze from their conversion perspective how they can "affect the quality of the day" in their particular situation. These men and women will be able to develop economic

## A Conscious Endeavor

relationships and establish business practices that are good for the planet and for human beings.

The person who is serious about his/her conversion has a reference point from which to consider what is going on around him/her. This reference point, i.e., the Judeo-Christian values from the Scriptures that we have been discussing in chapters 5 and 6, do not allow for the formation of a particular political party or a particular economic system that can be baptized as being Jewish or Christian. But this tradition does provide us with the tools to serve as a prophetic (constructively, critically, guiding) voice to help form societies that economically and politically function in ways that liberate the human spirit.

Societies are formed of people. Just as individual people go through a conversion process in their lives, so too our institutions (governmental, economic, educational) are constantly in need of conversion. Causing this institutional change (conversion) is the result of social/political involvement. That is why Emerson was right on point about a society benefiting nothing when individuals who are not themselves renovated attempt to renovate things around them. As we discuss economics and politics in the chapters that follow, we will be giving examples and raising questions that present issues for our common reflection.

It would be wrong to say we are not going to be critical of much that is going on. But we will not be critical without at the same time being hopeful. It does little only to point out what is wrong in the present situation without giving voice to other possibilities.

In the long run, the muse of the Judeo-Christian tradition is a voice of hope. It is a voice that calls to conversion but does not leave us feeling downtrodden. It is an approach to societal problems that starts with each of us examining ourselves, looking at where our soul needs to grow strong, and then applying that to all of our relationships.

At the same time, it is an approach that calls us to be a prophetic voice, to look honestly at the societal relationships that exist and point out where they are in need of change. In all cases the approach is one that yearns for the liberation of the human spirit. As Paul says:

> From the beginning till now the entire creation, as we know, has been groaning in one great act of giving birth; and not only creation; but all of us . . . groan inwardly as we wait for our bodies to be set free. (Rom 8:22–23)

# 8
# Property Rights

VERY EARLY ON IN the formation of the United States there was a concern expressed by its best thinkers about its unhealthy approach to property. Alexis de Tocqueville in his classic work *Democracy in America*, produced in stages between 1835 and 1848, said:

> If we attentively consider each of the classes of which society is composed, it is easy to see that the passions created by property are keenest and most tenacious among the middle classes.... The men who have a competency, alike removed from opulence and from penury, attach an enormous value to their possessions. As they are still almost within the reach of poverty, they see its privations near at hand and dread them; between poverty and themselves is nothing but a scanty fortune, upon which they immediately fix their apprehensions and their hopes.... No one is fully contented with his present fortune; all are perpetually striving in a thousand ways to improve it.... Do not talk to him of the interest and the rights of mankind; this small domestic concern absorbs for the time all his thoughts.[1]

And Emerson in his *Essay on Politics* wrote:

> There is an instinctive sense, however obscure and yet inarticulate, that the whole constitution of property, on its present tenures, is

---

1. Tocqueville, *Democracy in America*, 2:253–54. It is interesting that things have not changed much to this day. According to the National Low Income Housing Coalition in Washington, DC, 80 percent of the workers in the United States have only savings for six months if they lost their job today. This means that most of us are only six months from homelessness. This leads to a deep concern about job security and a preoccupation with our possessions.

injurious, and its influence on persons deteriorating and degrading; that truly the only interest for the consideration of the State is persons; that property will always follow persons; that the highest end of government is the culture of men; and that if men can be educated, the institutions will share their improvement and the moral sentiment will right the law of the land.[2]

I agree with Emerson. When attention is paid to the development of the inner person through education, then all society will benefit by the improvement of the individual. This idea is very reminiscent of the story of the story of Zacchaeus the tax collector in the Gospels. The inner renewal of one person benefits all those around him/her. Another example of this benefit of society by the change of the individual, which is also pointed towards a reflection of people on the material striving part of our lives, is Charles Dickens's *A Christmas Carol*. As Scrooge reflects on his past, present, and future, his inner changes create a difference in all of his relationships to people, and certainly to his relationship with his wealth. The emphasis on property and the rights of property is quite a sacred cow in Western society in general, and certainly in the United States. The emphasis that developed in the United States regarding property rights is perhaps epitomized in the Supreme Court decision of 1886 in the case of Santa Clara County vs. Southern Pacific Railroad. In this decision it was declared that a corporation is a natural person and therefore has all the rights declared under the Constitution and the Bill of Rights. I call attention to this case because it was at this point in United States history that corporate (and therefore property) rights took priority over the rights of the individual as a point of law. This extreme fascination with property and ownership bears critical reflection. While we have seen that ownership is important as a way of exercising stewardship and caring for the earth, our obsession with materialism and "having" has become destructive. There is a substantial number of people who place more value on money and property than on human life.

When I was in graduate school in Berkeley, California, in the late 60s and early 70s, protesting against the Vietnam War was something that partly defined my generation. East of Berkeley, in the city of Concord, there exists the Concord Naval Weapons Plant. It was from here that many bombs were shipped over to Vietnam. Of course, this plant became a focus

---

2. Emerson, *Selected Writings*, 380–81. Both de Tocqueville and Emerson wrote these selections in the 1840s. It is striking how similar their concerns about property are.

## Property Rights

of protest. One day a man named Brian Wilson decided to sit down in the railroad tracks to stop the train, now loaded with weapons being shipped to the Oakland shipping yards. I will never forget the newsreel showing the train ever so slowly run him over. They knew he was there and could have stopped. He survived even though both his legs were severed by the train wheels. I am not saying that Mr. Wilson should not have suffered some consequence for his civil disobedience. But to run over a human life to defend property seems a bit extreme to me. They could have stopped, had him arrested, and went along their way. This incident illustrates graphically just how out of whack things can get. As a touch of irony, most of the news stations and the talk shows were quite sympathetic to the train conductors. They felt Mr. Wilson got what was coming to him.

A newspaper article by Geraldine Fabrikant of the *New York Times* in 1996 about Ted Turner stated the case well:

> That is not to say Turner takes no notice of the size of his fortune. The investment in land, at $150 million roughly 5% of his assets, is not so large or so reckless as to jeopardize his place on the Forbes 400, a list he (Turner) has called a deterrent to charitable giving because those on it want to keep the wealth that put them there. Nonetheless, he conceded: "We're a nation of lists. People like to move up on lists. The first time I looked and saw my name, I thought, "Hmmmm, I can do a little better."[3]

Since the writing of that article, Mr. Turner has decided to distribute a large amount of his fortune and profits through a charitable donation to be given to the United Nations. This certainly signifies a profound change in Mr. Turner as he has reflected on the wealth he has amassed through his hard work. Mr. Turner has in many ways changed his relationship to wealth, and is using the proceeds of his labor to benefit those in very great need. Turner, in the aspect of the relationship to wealth, shows all the signs of a reflective man seeking inner change. There is something about our fascination with wealth and the power it brings that kills the spirit of stewardship and justice. As we discovered in our New Testament discussion, when our property is destructive of our inner spirit we need to do something to bring ourselves back into Right Relationship. This will involve conversion.

Historically, many human rights have been connected to property ownership, such as the right to vote. The relationship between property and rights has been such that rights invested in the individual by property

---

3. Fabrikant, "Don't Fence in Ted Turner or His Bison," 9B.

ownership have in many cultures superseded any rights that may be intrinsic to us by the very nature of being human. Thomas Jefferson refers to this reality in the Declaration of Independence. While he did not realize that he should also have been referring to women and slaves and Native Americans, not just European white males, he was right in realizing that all people are endowed by their creator with certain inalienable rights among which are "life, liberty, and the pursuit of happiness." A culture that says that rights are attached to property is saying that humans have value only insofar as they own something. Even though we act as if this were true, in our soul we know it is not.

It is at this very basic level that the Judeo-Christian tradition has a disagreement with most economic systems. The Judeo-Christian tradition does not give primacy to property as the basis of human rights. Rather, the tradition gives primacy to the dignity of the individual as a son or daughter of God. The Judeo-Christian tradition sees the dignity of humans rooted in their spiritual aspect, and it is from this that all rights flow.

It is because we are sons and daughters of God that we are placed in the role of stewards. We are given a role as stewards so we can actively play a role in caring for creation and in creating Right Relationships.

We recall that this role of stewardship, acknowledged by both the Old and New Testaments, was assured to every family every fifty years during the Year of Jubilees. The Year of Jubilees asserted an important truth: society functions best when the property is broadly distributed amongst all the people. In light of this tradition, men and women involved in the conversion process will question the wisdom of the concentration of wealth in the hands of the few.

Insofar as it is in our nature from God to be stewards, the ownership of property is acknowledged as a natural right. The right to own property flows out of our stewardship, and is not seen as an absolute in itself. In other words, the only purpose of having ownership is to exercise love and care for the earth, not so we can be full of avarice and pride about our possessions.

The novel *The Day the Cowboys Quit* by Elmer Kelton dramatizes an attempted strike by cowboys in Texas in 1883. At one point in his story, Kelton describes a meeting held by the large cattle ranchers to discuss how they might effectively break the strike. Mr. Selkirk, one of the new corporate cattle ranchers, has called the meeting. At one point he says to the group:

> Up and down the river are small squatters and that sort who dignify their position by calling themselves ranchers; in reality they

are maverick runners and cattle thieves. Then in these miserable nesterments that pass themselves off as towns are people who agitate against us. In short, Gentlemen, we stand against a motley array of ragtag enemies who represent a threat to the growth and security of this entire region. Whatever we do has to be calculated to clear the range once and for all of this obstructionist element. Until we, the substantial owners who have a bonafide investment in the future of this region, can control it and shut out these undesirables, there will be no security for us and our property.[4]

In many ways, the "taming of the West" repeated what occurred during the Enclosure Movement in England. By and large in the West, there was a taking of large open lands by the large ranchers and the railroads, who set themselves against the smaller landholders and those who were making a modest living off the land.

In Kelton's novel we see in the character Selkirk and most of the ranchers the attitude that the right to ownership does not extend beyond themselves; indeed, the making of law is even seen as their right by dint of their land ownership. They perceive people who own less than them as essentially having no rights. Another rancher says:

> The hell with state law; it's none of their business. We control the County law around here, and there ain't much anybody can do if we run our own courts. I say let's stretch some rope.[5]

The root of our problems with property ownership seems to begin when ownership is separated from stewardship. If we do not believe that all are called to stewardship, then we will not be concerned about a just distribution of wealth. We will not be concerned because we will not hold as a value all people having a relationship to ownership that allows them to practice stewardship. Our individual ownership must never preclude others' rights in this regard.

Ownership is a very emotional issue. Much of the reason for this emotion is a direct result of our lack of connection to our soul. A rancher was talking with his neighbor one day. He asked his neighbor, "If you had two houses and your neighbor had none, would you let him live in one of your houses?" The neighbor replied, "Yes." "Well," the rancher continued, "if you had two barns and your neighbor had none, would you let him use one of your barns?" Again, the neighbor replied, "Yes." Finally, the rancher

---

4. Kelton, *The Day the Cowboys Quit*, 52.
5. Ibid.

asked, "If you had two horses, and your neighbor had none, would you let him use one of your horses?" This time the neighbor answered, "Absolutely not!" Surprised, the rancher asked, "But why not?" The neighbor replied, "Because I do have two horses." It is easy for us to speak theoretically about how the goods of the earth should be shared if they are goods we do not have to share. The moment we talk about sharing what we really do have, many of us will cringe at the idea.

We seem to let ourselves be defined by our property instead of understanding that our relationship to our property is a temporary one. We will die. Our relationship to property is meant for us to come to an understanding of nurturing, of taking care of the earth. When we lose touch with this, a Right Relationship with property becomes less and less possible.

The land itself is for all of us to enjoy. We can say that the land is for the common good. Our right to ownership must be seen in light of the common good.

There are many who develop what can be called a fundamentalist view of property rights which says, "This is my property and I can do what I darn well please with it." What is wrong with this approach is that it leaves out the notion of the common good.

If, for instance, I wish to dump toxic chemicals on my property, this is certainly not for the common good, and I should not be allowed to do it. The "common good" argument has been used successfully both by governments and by citizen groups.

When many of the U.S. National Parks were formed, there was a public taking of land (the land was paid for, but eminent domain was applied). The preservation of certain types of geological formations, wild animal habitat, and/or particular types of trees/plants have often been viewed as for the greater common good. Recently, in Utah, federal lands were created to preserve canyon lands, against the protestations of the coal industry. This was certainly a case where the common good dictated the use of the stewardship of land against and directly opposed to a private interest.

Citizen groups have often banded together to prevent the storage of nuclear wastes in or near areas inhabited by human beings or areas where it could present a danger to other forms of life. Groups have formed to oppose certain types of development in order to preserve certain species of animals and plants. When done for disinterested, selfless reasons, such communal concerns are noble and for the common good.

# Property Rights

There is another relationship to property or land that we call patriotism. Some people tend to identify patriotism and nationalism. This should not be done.

Patriotism comes from the Latin word *patria*, which literally would be translated "fatherland." Many people have fond memories of the geographical area where they grew up. For me, Eugene, Oregon, and the surrounding Willamette Valley will always hold some magnetism. There is something about the land where I was born that will always have an archetypical pull on me. There is a beauty there that feels like home. This has also happened with me in areas where I have moved and lived for a long time. This kind of *patria*-tism has a lot of emotion connected to it. This is so because it involves a very real love of the land. Loving the land is exactly what we are supposed to do. Love of the land is a healthy and good thing.

Love for the land is different from the structure of government and economic system under which I live. Love for the land will assure that we will carry out our stewardship correctly. One will not deface, destroy, and ruin what one loves.

Thus, patriotism as love for the land should not be confused with or identified with nationalism. Nationalism is an emotional identity with a particular political system. Sometimes, as in the Germany of Hitler, it is also identified with a particular ethnic group. Then it is subtlety packaged and intermingled with elements of love of the land in a romantic and emotional way. This can be dangerous. For if you do not then fit the definition of what is patriotically acceptable, you can be purged. It is good to love the land. It is good to like the good things of our culture. (Every culture has enriching and dehumanizing aspects. We must learn to know the difference.) But when our culture is perceived as being better than others instead of just different and more familiar, we are in danger of becoming what I call nationalistic fundamentalists, i.e., "My country, right or wrong." This viewpoint destroys the human soul.

From the Judeo-Christian perspective, property ownership ought to be viewed from the standpoint of stewardship and the just distribution of wealth exemplified in the Year of Jubilees. The land is not something to be clung to as a possession, but something to be nurtured for the good of all men and women, and in thanksgiving to the creator.

In her novel *Animal Dreams*, Barbara Kingsolver has two of her characters—Cosima, a Mexican-American woman, and Loyd (the only Loyd

## A Conscious Endeavor

Cosima ever known with one L), an Apache, discuss the significance of the Pueblo Kachina dances. Loyd explains:

> [The Kachina dance] it's like the spirits have made a deal with us. . . . We're on our own. The spirits have been good enough to let us live here and use the utilities, and we're saying: we know how nice you're being. We appreciate the sun, we appreciate the deer we took. Sorry if we messed up anything. You've gone to a lot of trouble, and we'll try to be good guests.[6]

---

6. Kingsolver, *Animal Dreams*, 239–40.

# 9

# Distribution of Wealth and Just Wages

I DEVELOPED AFFORDABLE HOUSING for over twenty years in California. The work involved the production of affordable housing in both rural and urban areas.

There are a number of professional associations on the national, state, and local levels to which many in the affordable housing business belong. Two of these, the National Low Income Housing Coalition and the National Homeless Coalition, publish some interesting statistics.

One statistic is that approximately 80 percent of the workforce of the United States is only six months away from homelessness. This means if 80 percent of working-class families of the U.S. lost their jobs, they would only have sufficient savings to continue to make rent or mortgage payments for six months. After this they would be homeless. A fact like this makes the word of Alexis de Tocqueville in the last chapter even more sinister 175+ years after they were written. Many of us are very close to penury.

Another interesting fact is that most low-income households in the United States need to work two to three jobs at minimum wage in order to provide a roof over their heads. In many areas of the United States, a one-bedroom, one-bathroom apartment may rent for anywhere between $1,450 and $2,050 per month, with an average of $1,750 per month. If you add another $120 per month for gas and electricity, you have a monthly housing cost of $1,870 per month for housing alone. This would come to an annual housing cost of $22,400 per year.

Let us assume that a wage earner earns $9 per hour (many low-income people in the U.S. earn less than this). His or her annual income will be

103

$18,840. In this case housing cost clearly exceeds the annual income of a minimum wage earner working one job at forty hours per week.

In 1992 The United Nations Development Program (UNDP) stated that 20 percent of people in the wealthiest nations received 82.7 percent of the world's income. At the same time, only 1.4 percent of the world's income goes to the poorest 20 percent of people who live in the world's poorest countries.[1]

In 1989 in the United States, those in the top 1 percent of income earners received more total income than the bottom 40 percent. And in the same year the real income of the top 1 percent increased by 78 percent, whereas that of the bottom 20 percent decreased by 10.4 percent.[2]

I spoke earlier of the concentration of wealth in the hands of the few. Realities like these listed above have continued for years. We need to seriously analyze and consider the pros and cons of economic systems that perpetuate this lack of balance and fairness. Those who are in the upper 20 percent of world income need to understand that more often than not they live the lifestyle to which they have become accustomed at the expense of those who are in the bottom 40 percent of income. Only when we begin to not only understand, but accept this, will it be possible for us to undergo a conversion of our hearts and minds in relation to the production and the consumption of wealth.

In the 1990's Nike generated regular protests at the their corporate offices in Portland, Oregon. Nike was called a "network" or "outsource" firm then. In the United States they employed over 8,000 people in design, sales, and promotion, but the production of the actual shoes was accomplished by 75,000 workers in Indonesia and Vietnam. A pair of Nikes sold for $150 in the United States was then produced for about $5.40, and the workers who made them were paid as little as $0.15 per hour. These workers were housed in company barracks. Overtime was mandatory. There were no unions. When attempts were made to organize unions, the local military was employed to handle the problem. The $20 million that Nike paid to basketball great Michael Jordan in 1992 for endorsing Nike shoes exceeded the entire annual payroll of the men and women in the Indonesian factories who made them.[3] Since Nike contracts with independent labor contractors

---

1. Korten, *When Corporations Rule the World*, 106–7.

2. Ibid., 108–9.

3. Ibid., 111. Since the publishing of Korten's book, Nike has opened factories in Vietnam, where the same problems prevail.

in the outsource countries, they either deny that these practices exist or they say it is not their problem.

Nike continues to profit and new celebrities receive more than double what Michael Jordan was paid to endorse their line of shoes and products. The outsourced labor force continues to spread and the price for the top-selling Nike shoe continues to increase.

Internet usage has allowed ease of sharing current information. If you have an inquiring mind, the information is out there. You just have to let it in. A current Internet search on working conditions and wages of outsourced workers reveal improvements, yet wages remain considerably low in comparison to the cost of the products produced. This spread between Nike's cost of production and their sales prices in the U.S. and Western Europe allows them to continue to pour vast amounts of dollars into advertising and promotion of their products through university and college sports teams and more traditional advertising outlets. Nike remains a cultural icon.

The statement "Well, at least, some work is being provided to the people in developing nations that was not being provided before" is commonly used when rationalizing the industrialization and outsourcing of Third World countries. But we forget they have two serious effects.

First, the industrialization that continues to occur throughout the world destroys agricultural land. The destruction or change in use of many agricultural lands drives many families out of agricultural areas to the cities in order to find work. When one compares the quality of the agricultural life they had before to the squalor and lack experienced by displaced families in an urban environment, we see their quality of life has diminished. For every convenience, there is an inconvenience.

Similarly, a reality we have seen dramatically played out in Central America is the change of agricultural use of land from food staples such as grain, small farm animal husbandry, and vegetable production to non-staple food production for export (such as Chiquita bananas or McDonalds raising vast herds of cattle in Chile and Argentina). The result is land that used to be used for farms that could support a smaller family is no longer available for this purpose. Thus migration from rural to urban areas, such as begun in Europe and the United States in the last century, continues in Africa, our world's remaining untapped agricultural land.

The wages these workers are paid are not sufficient to support them and their families in an urban setting. One can see comparisons with what happened to immigrant families in the United State from the Civil War period to the First World War with the rise of industrial capitalism in the New England region of the United States, in particular. Walter Rauschenbusch, a Presbyterian minister who worked in New York with immigrant families living in squalor in tenements, attests to this reality in many of his writings.

I have seen the passage of free trade agreements—NAFTA and GATT. The theory of these free trade agreements was essentially the "trickle down" theory: if Third World Country X produces goods for First World Country B, those in Third World Country X are automatically better off because jobs are created. When Ronald Reagan was president of the United States, he encouraged this philosophy of economics. His own Vice President Bush called this "voodoo economics," and it was proven to not work in reality. If the company or corporation involved in free trade in a Third World Country were concerned about just wages and the environmental effects of their production both socially (effects on culture) and on the physical environment, such trade agreements could be a good thing. If true development of the underdeveloped nation were at the forefront of the foreign corporation, then a real distribution of wealth would occur. A creation of a middle class would develop. And an environment that allowed for healthy social development in a new economic atmosphere could emerge—one that would strengthen the existing cultural fabric instead of contributing to its destruction. But more often than not, Third World countries are viewed as resources of cheap labor and cheap resources (raw materials), and exploitation occurs instead of true development.

Let's look at results of GATT in Mexico. The maquiladoras across the border of Texas, Arizona, and California have created production plants built by U.S.-based corporations that are not subject to the environmental laws of the United States. The spinoff has been polluted streams, toxic wastes, and the development of health problems for workers in these plants and those living in proximate communities. Likewise, Mexico City has become the most polluted city on the planet, and Rio de Janeiro is not far behind. Both have been overrun by rural-to-urban migration and an industrialization that has not been regulated with a care for the environment or for the true social development of those countries. Trickle down economics does not work for the good of all.

This story has been repeated in different global locations for many different products consumed by those in the upper 20 percent of income. Much of it is clothing production, auto production, and manufacturing of electronic components. The stories come from China, Taiwan, Korea, Indonesia, Mexico, Central America . . . stories of work outsourced by corporations where workers are paid much less than in the U.S. and Europe. When workers complain or try to form unions to improve wages and working conditions, the local government military is used to control these attempts by workers to unionize.

Hearing about examples of outsourcing and the conditions of industrialization instills a feeling of helplessness. If we do not strive to educate ourselves about the facts, it becomes impossible for us to figure out a process of personal conversion, and ultimately the conversion of our economic system, to one in which people matter more than profits. At the same time it becomes impossible for us to break through our complacency to figure out how to work with others in the political or economic process to stop injustices that exist.

A strategy I could take would be to simply stop buying Nike shoes, but this act would not in itself stop Nike's business practices regarding outsourcing. But the boycott of Nike products is a moral decision one might make as an individual. If one could get all those in wealthy nations to stop buying Nike shoes, this would certainly get attention and force Nike to re-evaluate and perhaps even put an end to business practices that adversely impact contracted production workers. This type of strategy was used to exert pressure on South Africa to end Apartheid. When wealthy nations and their investors collectively withdrew investments in companies with holdings in South Africa, the political and financial pressure led to the end of Apartheid.

There are other actions citizens who live in consumer nations can do to promote justice at home and in the developing nations where consumer products are produced.

Let us turn now to examining the just wage issue in a United States context. Perhaps there are assumptions we can draw from this examination that we can transfer to our examination of practices presently occurring in developing nations.

When one looks back historically at basic societal structures, we see that the family is the most basic societal unit. The family has been based on three models: tribe (pre-industrial), extended family (pre-industrial/rural), and nuclear family. The family is so basic to a society's health that when family structures disintegrate, societies disintegrate.

## A Conscious Endeavor

In our own history, as the American government broke down tribal structures of the American Indian, their societal structures failed. Obviously, this was done intentionally. Whether the failure of the family structure is brought about intentionally, or unintentionally as the byproduct of "progress," we must evaluate whether the societal deterioration produced as a result is tolerable and/or acceptable.

For example, when I was a young child in the 1950s I remember hearing stories about Russia. One of the stories I often heard was about children who were reared in babysitting collectives while both parents worked. I remember hearing a general discussion by adults of what a terrible thing this was. Yet today in the urban areas of the United States most children are raised in daycare centers and at school. The norm is that either both parents work or there is a one-parent family (approximately 40 percent of the families in the U.S. today have one parent). In most urban areas, the "extended family" is non-existent.

Both parents working has been the U.S. experience since the 1970s, and there is a general consensus that the resulting breakdown of the family has not been good for family life or for our society at large. David Korten states poignantly:

> Parents are so busy working (both parents) that they are left with little time, energy, or encouragement to do more than function as wage earners and night guardians. The modern urban home has become little more than a place to sleep and watch television.[4]

American family structures have been breaking down for some time and the American family is failing. This is not a desirable situation. Since the family is such a basic societal structure, we cannot expect to have society function in a healthy manner if one of its most basic structures is disintegrating.

Not unlike most other cultures, in the Judeo-Christian cultural traditions the family unit has been very important. For it is through this structure that the values (faith) of the parents and of the group are passed on to the children. The family structure is the place where, in a sense of real faith, people will learn about their dignity as sons and daughters of God, and by extension, the dignity of all people. It is in the family that children learn honesty, fairness, justice, and love. If not there, then often they do not learn these things at all. Providing a strong family upbringing for children

---

4. Ibid., 45.

is a real commitment on the part of adults. In some cultures, the raising of children is a shared responsibility, and in many rural areas of the United States where communities are smaller and where extended families are more common, there is often a more extended-family approach to the raising of children. However, in our urban and suburban environments this extended family is often missing. One of the results is that we see more of a nuclear family approach to childrearing. In addition, with the higher rate of divorce, we often see one parent raising a child or children with little or no communal or extended-family support. This has made it particularly difficult both for parents and for children.

I remember as I grew up I spent about 80 percent of my time around adults. There were my parents, of course, but in addition there were many other adults—close friends of my parents—who became extended family. As I entered adolescence I had other adults who were not my parents who I could talk to about things. I am sure that most of the time these other adults gave me the same advice my parents would have given me, but since they were not "authority figures" I was more open to what they had to say, or they would reinforce what my parents had already said, thus making me more open to what my parents had to offer in the way of advice.

I have noticed that today, especially in urban and suburban environments, children are left to themselves most of the time. This is most likely because parents have to work just to put bread on the table and a roof over their heads. Or it may be that both parents work because they feel they want to live a certain "material" lifestyle. Many wants over time become needs, and there are people who begin to feel that they just can't get along without certain things. And that is all they are—things. Do two people really need a 3,500 square-foot home, a pool, an athletic club membership, and three cars? It is rather easy to convince yourself that you do.

Children are not getting the loving attention they need. When I lived in Colorado, a stone's throw from the town of Littleton, the tragedy occurred at Columbine High School. The parents of Derrick Kliebold said they had absolutely no idea that their son was building bombs in their garage, or that he had guns and bomb makings in his bedroom. The parents lived in a very respectable middle-class suburban neighborhood.

It has been interesting to note that with children having no adults to talk to, they turn to each other for advice. And what do they know? Not much. I have hit my late sixties, and I am amazed at how little I know. It frightens me that young children, adolescents, and young adults often have no adult to bounce things off of. It is not so much that adults have some magical kind of knowledge and that young people know nothing. But if an adult has lived any type of reflective life and learned how to think critically he or she can bring that insight to younger people. And when a younger person wants to discuss their music, or the pressures they are feeling from their peers, and all the confusion, troubles, hurts, and pains they face, an adult can help them think critically and can give them nurturing and love. They can show the younger person that no matter how hard life might seem, they can make it through the rough times with a sense of hope and dignity and be better off for it.

In a Judeo-Christian context, one of the purposes of the family is to provide a loving environment in which the individual can grow to loving maturity, become critical of what he or she sees around them, accept and support what is good, and stay away from or even fighting against what is bad. One aspect of the Judeo-Christian perspective on childrearing is that it is a real commitment, and that an adult should be around children during the period of their growing into adulthood.

Therefore, since the Judeo-Christian approach to family over the years has evolved into one in which consistent adult attention in the home during the time of the children being raised is of utmost importance, when we have a discussion about wages we must discuss total household income in which, ideally, only one of the parents works outside the home. It might be the husband or the wife, but ideally only one of them will work outside the home during the period children are being reared.

Raising a family is a commitment, and not only the individuals in the family must make this commitment. Society must also make a commitment that will allow the family to function. In 1993 the Family Leave Act in the United States was passed. The following year the Family Friendly Leave Act expanded leave usage of sick leave for family members. The legislation stepped towards this commitment to family.

A just wage would be the most appropriate way to assure the strength of the family. A just wage would be paid to one person who would be the wage earner for his or her household. This wage would address some basic rights of families to which all families are entitled. This wage will allow one adult to be home providing the adult example, supervision, instruction, and consistent love to children so necessary to the development of healthy, loving human beings.

## Distribution of Wealth and Just Wages

One of the charismatic religious leaders of our time was Pope John XXIII. In 1963 he wrote a letter called *Peace on Earth* in which he described some of the basic rights people have. He and others have said these rights include: bodily integrity; the means suitable for the proper development of life; food; clothing; shelter; rest; medical care; necessary social services; security in cases of sicknesses, inability to work, old age, or unemployment; and the right to share in the benefits of culture, that is, the basic right to education and technical professional training in keeping with the stage of educational development in the country to which he/she belongs.[5]

Often discussions of a just wage sum up well the Judeo-Christian concerns: food, clothing, housing, medical care, health insurance, care in old age, and a share in the benefits of the culture, particularly education. Presented in the following table is the monthly income needed to provide a family the basic rights addressed by John XXIII in his letter. These figures assume a household of three living in a two-bedroom apartment in an average metropolitan area of the United States.

| | |
|---|---|
| Rent | $1,750 |
| Utilities/renter's insurance | 450 |
| Phone/Internet | 425 |
| Clothing | 150 |
| 1 auto plus insurance & fuel | 849 |
| Health coverage | 1400 |
| Food | 640 |
| Entertainment | 250 |
| Savings | 400 |
| Monthly total | $6,324 (2014 U.S. dollars) |
| Annual total | $75,888 |

If we assume that there are 2,080 work hours in a year (52 weeks times 40 hours per week), then a just wage computes to be somewhere around $36.50 per hour. Presently the minimum wage in the United States is $7.25 and California's minimum wage is $9.00—hardly a just wage. The hourly wage quoted above may sound upsetting to many employers. If it is, let them examine the budget carefully and point out any extravagances.

---

5. Pope John XXIII, *Peace on Earth*, 11–13.

## A Conscious Endeavor

I was involved in real estate development for many years. I always hired a union signatory general contractor. I knew he would hire union subcontractors. I knew I could set my head on the pillow each night knowing everyone involved on my job sites got a just wage. Many jobs received federal or state tax dollars that required Davis-Bacon wage reporting with each month's construction draw. While filling out the forms was horrendous, it did assure just wages. And while many in the construction industry complained about the paperwork, some realized that the guarantee of just wages it provided was important.

Often it may take a government program or tax dollars in combination with private dollars to pay just wages. There is nothing wrong with this. When one looks at a just wage ultimately as an investment in strong families and a stronger society, the investment tends to have greater worth than can be measured in mere dollars and cents.

Justice is an obligation we all have. We are not talking about minimum subsistence. We are talking about an approach to labor and just wages that strengthens the family, and therefore the whole society. We cannot look at the value of labor in a depersonalized way or separated from the reality of how labor affects the family.

Perhaps we need to begin asking ourselves whether the pricing of products we consume is so important that we do not mind if the result is destroyed families, with the social deterioration that normally follows destroyed families, i.e., higher crime, lower educational levels, and less distributive justice. We can't have it both ways.

The rich and the super-rich are able to insulate themselves from the darker realities that occur in societies when there is a lack of justice. Westchester, New York; Marin County, California; Scottsdale, Arizona . . . it seems every metropolitan area has exclusive neighborhood areas that protect the occupants of their residents from the perceived dangers of the general populace. People who live in these more privileged communities can become insular in their thinking.

Until we begin to see there is a direct relationship between a just wage and a better society, we will not fit this idea into the equation of land, labor, and capital. You will recall reading in chapter 6 from Matthew's Gospel the wonderfully poetic passage that talks about the lilies of the field. Part of what the passage is saying is we are not meant to have an obsessive relationship to our basic life needs. Lower income people are always having to worry about how they are going to pay the rent. This is not how life ought to be. People should be able to spend time with their families in a joyful manner. They should be able to help their children with their homework and take walks in the park.

The tensions caused by the culture of poverty are terribly destructive to the human spirit. I experienced this during the time I was chaplain of the Los Angeles County Jail, and I have seen it in over twenty years of providing affordable housing for low-income households. The culture of poverty denies a sense of hope and security to people. It makes them feel their lives have no value. The tensions caused in families by poverty often curtail or smother the love and nurturing that families are meant to provide.

When we do not pay just wages now, we end up paying more later. The lives broken by the culture of poverty can lead to crime and despair. Families broken and devalued by injustice often respond violently to the injustices done to them. The result is an increase in violent crime. Our current solution to this increase is to build more prisons. In California, since 1980 so many prisons have been built that the state cannot afford to adequately staff them. Another response to the perception of increased violence is the hiring of more police. We think this will control violence.

By contrast, the Judeo-Christian approach is that if we practice justice now, we will be blessed with peace within our borders. Peace is the gift justice brings. We have not spent enough time really thinking this through. When people are not treated justly, violence is being done to them. And this begins a spiral of violence that ends up in real loss of life through the physical violence that erupts in the culture of poverty. We must stop the spiral of violence where it begins: injustice. Not at the end, where it has already escalated into physical violence—murder, rape, and mayhem.

In the long run, just wages are probably cheaper than the costs to society suffered by the tolerance of injustice. It is time for us to take upon ourselves this work of justice in relationship to wages. It can actually be a happy task.

# 10

# Environmentalism

IN HIS POEM "ANTHEM," cowboy poet Buck Ramsey writes:

> It was the old ones with me riding
> Out through the fog fall of the dawn,
> And they would press me to deciding
> If we were right or we were wrong.
> For time came we were punching cattle
> For men who knew not spur nor saddle,
> Who came with locusts in their purse
> To scatter loose upon the earth.
> The savage men had not found this prairie
> Till some who hired us came this way
> To make the grasses pay and pay
> For some raw greed no wise and wary
> Regard for grass could satisfy.
> The old ones wept, and so did I.[1]

The last line of the poem makes it clear the writer has a great love of nature and the cowboy life. Otherwise, how could he weep at what is happening?

The basis of the whole Judeo-Christian ethic is love. We cannot talk about the environment outside of the context of love.

I ask you to call to mind someone you love very deeply. It might be a spouse, a child, a relative, or a friend. Imagine how you would feel if that person were treated without respect, debased in some way, or brutally mutilated beyond recognition. Believe it or not, we actually mutilate and debase

---

1. In Cannon, *New Cowboy Poetry*, 99–102.

## Environmentalism

the earth. But as we mentioned earlier, we are supposed to be stewards who love the earth. A steward takes care of something for someone else.

If we don't think of the earth with love and respect, a fruitful discussion of the environment is impossible. Francis of Assisi wrote a poem entitled "The Canticle of Brother Sun" in which he says:

> All praise by yours, my Lord, through all that you have made,
> And first my Lord Brother Sun,
> Who brings the day, and light you give to us through him . . .
> All praise be yours, my Lord, through Brothers Wind and Air,
> And fair and stormy, and all the weather's moods,
> By which you cherish all that you have made.
> All praise be yours, my Lord, through Sister Water,
> So useful, lowly, precious and pure is she . . .[2]

The Judeo-Christian tradition sees our relationship to the earth as including a spiritual aspect. For it is here, within the womb of the earth, that we are tasked to work out our conversion. As we mentioned in our Old Testament discussion, we are fellow creatures who share the earth. We have been given the honored role of stewards.

I am not recommending a naive and overly romanticized view of nature. I am recommending a very real love of the earth.

About ten years ago I was reading an article in *National Geographic* about the Amish in Pennsylvania. One of the observations in the article that stuck in my mind was that Amish grain, vegetable, and fruit yields from farming were from ten to twelve times the yield of corporate agricultural, which employs heavy equipment and nitrate and phosphate chemicals—such firms as ConAgra, Cargill, Tenneco, and ADM.

The Amish do not use any of these things, and they get yields of great magnitude. They have a Right Relationship with farming. The article explained how heavy equipment compacts soil and does not allow as much air to the root systems. Pesticides often kill more than the specific pest they target. And because of the leeching of the soil by rains, these chemicals end up in aquifers as well as the surface run off to streams, rivers, and ultimately oceans. Natural balances get upset. The nitrogen-rich soil produced by plowing, manure spreading, and composting seem more efficacious than fertilizers produced from chemicals.

Our relationship to the earth has become too materialistic and mechanistic. But the idea of loving the earth is not a materialistic idea. It is a

---

2. Quoted from Francis of Assisi, *St. Francis of Assisi*, 130–31.

spiritual idea. When we discussed the idea of conversion in chapters 3 and 4, we mentioned the Judeo-Christian model of social change as one of social change through personal conversion (change of the inner self). Thus, the Judeo-Christian approach will include at its center the social-change-through-conversion model when the person from this tradition considers his/her attitude towards nature and the use of the earth and its fruits for human sustenance.

When I was living in Utah I visited the Kennecott Copper Mine, perhaps the largest open pit mine in the world, certainly the largest in the United States. The literature available to tourists stated that where the mile-deep open pit is today used to stand a mountain a mile high. The mining company had literally ground a mountain into powder, and has gone a mile deep besides. One has to wonder about this wresting from the earth in such great amounts.

In California there exists a huge water project consisting of aqueducts as large as rivers that carry water from the Feather, Sacramento, and Stockton Rivers in the north of the state down to the San Joaquin Valley, the richest agricultural valley in the world.

The water project was funded through federal and state tax dollars. The original intent of the aqueduct system was to bring sufficient water to the valley to encourage small family farms. Originally no farm was to be larger than 160 acres.

Agribusiness figured out a way to get around the law, resulting in the eventual elimination of small family farms. Corporations like Tenneco, Sunkist, Lindsay, and others have taken over the valley with water funded by the taxpayer.

Another example: In Eugene, Oregon, where I grew up in the 1940s and 1950s, there were a number of small logging outfits who applied select cutting methods. When you "select cut," you select trees of only a certain size to cut. When you have finished logging a particular area, there was still an intact forest. Since the 1960s the small loggers have been replaced by large corporations that clearcut the forests. Clearcutting means exactly what it says. You clear an area. There is no forest left when you are finished. They call this "harvesting" the lumber. Had these logging companies planted the lumber, "harvest" would be an appropriate term, as in "You reap what you sow." But most of these trees grew up two to three hundred years ago. More truthfully, they are robbing a natural resource.

## Environmentalism

There are some logging companies that actually do harvest trees they planted twenty years ago, which average eight to twelve inches in diameter. These trees do not begin to compare with the giant trees that have been destroyed and "harvested." My point is not that trees should never be cut down. But select cutting of trees preserves a forest by cultivating an attitude that preserves the forest and the living area for other creatures. It assures a steady supply of larger growth and more efficient production of oxygen. This approach leans more towards stewardship than does the clearcutting approach.

The idea of clearcutting brings to mind the economic impacts of how we use our resources on public lands. The clearcutting of lumber in the Northwest United States has often occurred on National and State Forest lands. Usually these lands are administered by the National Forest Service or the state Bureau of Land Management, agencies originally established to manage these resources for the public interest. Over the years, these agencies have become managed at the political whim of whatever political party is in the White House. And too often these nationally and state-managed lands are used for purposes of political payoff or favoritism. Often the result is that corporations that log these lands get raw trees at a discount price at the public's expense.

Another example for our discussion is corporations that conduct mining on nationally or state-owned lands at a discount. When Bruce Babbitt, then Secretary of the Interior, thought the mining industry should pay a fair price for gold and silver mined on public lands, and that they should be required to restore the land to a satisfactory state after their mining efforts, the mining companies called this unreasonable and left-wing.

A final example we will bring up is ranchers who range cattle on national and state-owned lands. These ranchers are using grazing lands at a cost that does not reflect its true value. Again, I am not saying necessarily that grazing should not be allowed on public lands. But when ranchers are getting grazing lands at a discounted rate, we should call it what is: a cattle ranching welfare program. It might be true that it is important for the federal government to subsidize the farming and the ranching industries so that the general public can procure food at an affordable rate. This can be a good thing. But it is important to state clearly what we are doing and why we are doing it.

In the construction of single-family and apartment homes, in which I have been involved for over twenty years, the developer must buy the land, get it subdivided, build the streets, and build the homes. For each stage there is a cost, which becomes part of the sale price of the home. All the developer's real costs are part of his product, including whatever profit he might make. When you pay for every step of your production, including the raw material you are using, this is called "cost internalization." This condition is basic enough to market theory that it is rarely disputed even by doctrinaire free-market ideologues. If any part of the cost of the product is shared by a third party who in no way participates in any benefit from the transaction, then economists say that this cost has been "externalized." The child who uses his parents' table, pitcher, glasses, lemonade, sugar, and ice to set up his lemonade stand has externalized all of his costs except for labor (he or she must sit at the lemonade stand and sell the lemonade). To the extent that we externalize costs, the price of our product is distorted accordingly. Another way to say it is this: every externalized cost involves privatizing a gain and socializing its associated costs onto the community.[3] A simpler way to state this is: externalizing costs means the public is paying for profits that inure to the benefit of one or very few individuals.

The cases of agribusiness in California using water paid for by taxpayers and foresting, mining, and grazing on public lands are all examples of externalization of costs. And more often than not there is a social cost involved. A country can lose forever all its older trees. Serious erosion and destruction of streams, rivers, and fresh water life often result from clearcutting. Later generations often have to live with the toxic results of mine tailings, erosion, and the destruction to wildlife caused by the use of arsenic in gold mining.

I am bringing up the idea of cost externalization in this discussion for two reasons: 1. In cost externalization a profiteer takes a profit from a product he did not create or pay for. 2. There is always a cost to the public, whether immediately or later. Usually there is a cost now *and* later.

The water project in California gives us an example of costs absorbed by the public both now and later. When the water project was built in California, water from the Feather, Sacramento, and Stockton Rivers was diverted from the San Pablo/San Francisco Bays into the aqueduct system.

Imagine the bay as a place where the ocean (salt water) and the rivers (fresh water) meet. The force of the fresh water coming from the rivers kept the salt water towards the west end of the San Francisco Bay, even at high tide. With the diversion of this water into the aqueduct system, and the resulting

---

3. Korten, *When Corporations Rule the World*, 76.

## Environmentalism

lack of flow pressure from the three rivers pushing into the bays, the salt water came all the way up into San Pablo Bay. Various cities in the East Bay of the San Francisco Bay Area drew their drinking water from the east side of San Pablo Bay. They now find they have an alkali/salinity problem with their drinking water. Not only has agribusiness externalized its water costs, which gives them cheap water to grow produce, but also a social/health problem has direct resulted from this externalization of costs. Did we know when these canals were originally built that all these things would happen? Probably not. Because so often our decisions are made with short-terms gains and short-term needs, and short-term political considerations putting pressure on the decision making process, we do not take the time to reflect carefully on the implications of our present decisions and actions.

We will speak of externalization of costs on an international level later. But we can see clearly, in the potential damage to our own natural resources, what externalization of costs in the interest of immediate profits, or immediate satisfaction of what is perceived as serious present needs, can produce.

We know there is only one earth. There is only so much land, air, water . . . all our natural resources are limited. We know that what makes it possible for us to breathe is the production of oxygen through the process of photosynthesis. We know trees are the most efficient plant at making oxygen. Yet we continue clearcutting trees in the U.S., South America, and Africa as if there were no limit to this resource. And for what? For short-term corporate profits.

We know there is only so much water on the earth. We know that our own bodies are upwards of 80 percent water. We know our bodies need to be constantly hydrated by drinking water, or else we will die. We know that what goes into the water will ultimately go into our bodies. But for some reason we treat profits as more important than our own lives. This is a clear example of thought processes gone completely awry.

In the Judeo-Christian Scriptures it is very clear that our main purpose for existence is not profit at any cost. We might involve ourselves in enterprises that do make profits, but profit is secondary to justice and stewardship. This is the difficult world in which persons seeking inner conversion find themselves. This is the world in which we must work out our conversion with integrity.

I have reread works by Adam Smith, Ricardo, Malthus, Keynes, Friedman, and Galbraith. There is an assumption that runs through all of them: the economy can and must keep growing; capital and profits must ever be on the increase. This thinking assumes there is an infinite amount of materials that will keep fueling the economy of which they speak. But there isn't. We must find a way to steward the earth in a balanced way, and build an economy that promotes the greatest benefits to the earth, its resources, and to human beings.

As we discussed in chapter 5, the Judeo-Christian view is that we are stewards. Being a steward is essentially taking care of something for someone else. We have been given this sacred trust. We ought not take our responsibilities lightly. Stewardship calls for reverence and meticulous concern in every detail of how we use the earth's resources.

I find it interesting that people who are environmentally sensitive are made to feel they lack rationality. It seems more often than not when long-term environmental sensitivity is in conflict with short-term profits, the profit motive is seen as the more rational and responsible view.

When the Clinton Administration placed southern Utah canyon lands under federal protection, the act was viewed by most people in Utah merely from the standpoint of loss of potential profits and jobs.

Environmentalists in California who want to prevent the placement of dams on the Eel River to protect it as a wilderness are seen as unreasonable by those who want to harness the power of the river with dams and convert it to electricity to be sold for profit.

The members of the ship Green Peace are seen as a bunch of loonies. Why is it that those who want to preserve the earth for future generations (remember the seven-generations approach of the Iroquois?) are considered the enemy? I am puzzled by this. I am not saying they are always right, but their voice and what they are trying to say will bring balance to our discussions. If they are not listened to with attention (remember obedience?) then our discussions surrounding the environment will lack balance, and our decisions will lack balance.

Today corporations speak of downsizing. More often than not this means increasing the use of robotics, computers, and outsourced labor. This results in laying off large numbers of employees. The resulting savings are usually given in salary increases to the top levels of management.

I do not agree with this concept of downsizing. I am convinced that for the good of the earth we need to start downsizing our businesses into modules that are both humanly and environmentally more sound.

We already know, for instance, that if there had been a large number of family farms created in the agricultural economy of California, there would be much greater employment. It would have taken no more subsidy than the present corporations are receiving. But instead of this subsidy going into the hands of a few, it would have been spread around more equally, provided more employment, and more family stability.

An additional effect of having many smaller farms instead of large corporate farms is that we would have more people involved in the production of our food who were paying attention to the whole process of agricultural production and husbandry. This would make a difference. When more people are involved in the process of the production of food, i.e., what we are going to be putting into our bodies, it is likely we will develop better food. There is certainly no proof that corporate farming produces a cheaper product than family farms. There is proof that corporate farming production methods have bad side effects and concentrate wealth in the hands of the few. It almost goes without saying that those of us who remember going to our parents or grandparents' farms and eating the corn or tomatoes they produced were tastier than what we can buy in the local supermarket.

Stewardship will involve a lot of listening, which, as we discussed earlier, is really what obedience is. In the Book of Job, Job says:

> If you would learn more, ask the cattle,
> seek information from the birds of the air.
> The creeping things of the earth will give you lessons,
> and the fishes of the sea will tell you all.
> There is not one such creature but will know
> this state of things is all of God's own making.
> He holds in his power the soul of every living thing,
> and the breath of each man's body. (12:7–10)

Our ability to name things is really a looking into, a listening to, and seeing relationships in nature. It is this active listening that allows us to practice good stewardship. It is this listening to other creatures, to nature itself, to whole ecosystems that will tell us whether or not what we are doing is in balance.

# 11
## Classical Economic Theory

IN 1776 TWO IMPORTANT events occurred in western culture and history. The American Revolution occurred, and Adam Smith published *The Wealth of Nations*. The Revolution and Adam Smith were dealing with similar issues in very different ways.

During the seventeenth century in England, the idea of the corporation was established. Prior to this time, owners were personally liable for the failures of their business enterprises. As discovery of the New World occurred, England allowed the formation of corporations for enterprises that were in the public (the crown's) interest. These corporations were tightly controlled by the crown. Their ventures were considered to be of high risk. The corporation was an entity that could minimize that risk.

When the colonies were established in America, they were established as corporations by charter of the king. There were certain rules governing corporations. While the colonies could be a source of raw materials for England, they were not allowed to manufacture goods. Raw materials were to be sent to England where manufacturing would occur. Some of these manufactured goods were then sent to the colonies to be sold.

Raw goods from the colonies were transformed into manufactured goods in England. This production was the basis of wealth and profits.

Both Smith and the early colonists saw the unfairness of this system. The colonists revolted against it and Smith saw no use for corporations. He thought both governments and corporations would suppress competition in the market.[1] Given that corporations in his day were very

---

1. Korten, *When Corporations Rule the World*, 55ff.

tightly controlled by the crown, it is possible to see how some arbitrary regulation would interfere.

The world of Adam Smith, David Ricardo, and Thomas Malthus was one that had seen the Enclosure Movement in England. This movement was initiated by wealthy landowners and ended tenant farming in rural England. Legal boundaries for properties were described and fences were placed. Anyone who was not a direct employee of the landowner was dismissed. Enclosure caused a substantial relocation of populations from rural to urban centers. Relocation provided a large source of unemployed people to rising industrial enterprises in the urban areas of England and Scotland in the eighteenth century.

This is the historical backdrop against which the classical economic thinkers reflected. Interestingly, these great thinkers were reflecting on what was actually occurring. They did not create an economic system. They made astute observations on the way goods were being produced, exchanged, and how capital was being employed. They analyzed the existing system, pointing to its strengths and weaknesses.

The classical economists were moving in a world in which the corporation was not yet the primary agency of conducting business. The norm was the family business.

Common themes run through Smith, Malthus, Ricardo, and most of the classical economic thinkers. One common thread is that the driving forces of the market are self-interest and competition. A second is that labor is a commodity in the marketplace. The classical economic thinkers observed how labor had become depersonalized. Depersonalization made it more possible to consider wages for labor in terms in terms of subsistence rather than in terms of justice. If you are talking about a commodity (labor) instead of laborers (real people), then justice (a right relationship between real people) is easily dropped from the discussion, and soon from the equation of wages altogether.

## SELF-INTEREST AND COMPETITION

For the classical economists (and for people like Milton Friedman today) the driving forces of the market were self-interest and competition. They had a firm faith that the interplay of these forces would work toward the common good because self-interest would get people to produce something people wanted, and competition would assure that it was produced at a price people were willing to pay. It was assumed the two would always temper one another. As Smith said:

> It is not from the benevolence of the butcher, the brewer, or the baker that we expect our dinner, but from regard to their own self interest.[2]

The idea of self-interest, and with it the idea that a person should constantly strive to better one's material lot as the primary quest in life, are modern notions. It is alien to the great lower and middle strata of Egyptian, Greek, Roman, and medieval cultures.[3]

I have been involved in what one would call idealistic endeavors for a long time. I have realized that, while it is indeed delightful when I witness a person or group commit themselves to something noble for purely idealistic, unselfish reasons, most of the time one must appeal to peoples' greed in order to get them involved in something that might also be idealistic in nature. I have found that in order to get people to consider the common good, more often than not you must show them what they are going to get for themselves in return. In the 1980s, I was working with a non-profit housing development corporation providing affordable housing in Marin County, California. It is known that Marin County is an enclave of some of the wealthiest people in the San Francisco Bay Area. Getting them to see the need for affordable housing for lower-income people was a challenge at every turn. Most of the time, local jurisdictions really did not want affordable housing in their neighborhoods. In 1982 one of the most severe winter storm systems hit northern California, including the Bay Area. Freeways were at times under six feet of water. It was then that people discovered that their police and fire protection employees were often commuting from the northern Santa Rosa area, where housing was more affordable, and were now not available to help people in emergency situations. All of a sudden communities in Marin County began to see affordable housing as something in their self-interest.

When Jesus sent some people forth to announce the Kingdom of God, he said, "Remember, I am sending you out like sheep among wolves; so be cunning as serpents and yet harmless as doves." (Matt 10:16). He is warning them not to be naive about what makes people tick.

---

2. Smith, *Wealth of Nations*, 213, quoted in Korten, *When Corporations Rule the World*, 56.

3. Heilbroner, *Worldly Philosophers*, 25.

## Classical Economic Theory

Adam Smith and others of his time saw this as well.

The question we need to ask ourselves from a Judeo-Christian perspective is: What is legitimate self-interest and what is raw greed? The two are not the same.

Legitimate self-interest should be thought of as corresponding to individual rights. All of us have a natural interest in procuring for ourselves what we perceive as our God-given/natural rights (Jefferson would refer to these as "inalienable rights" in the Declaration): respect for our dignity, food, clothing, shelter, happiness, freedom. To act in accordance with procuring these rights for ourselves is legitimate self-interest as long as we realize that we have the responsibility to recognize these rights as belonging to others as well. As we pursue rights for ourselves, we have the corresponding duty to make sure they are not obtained at the expense of negating these same rights for others.

Raw greed does not have this concern. Greed is an obsessive yearning to have, own, possess, and have power over. It does not concern itself with its effects on others beyond immediate control. Greed concerns itself only with whether or not the goal is accomplished, whether or not the desired end is achieved. Greed accompanies a desire for power gone awry. To have the power to obtain one's legitimate rights is one thing. To have the power to possess merely for the power of possessing, or merely to increase power over others, is quite another. Walter Lippmann once said about corporate executives:

> They have been educated to achieve success; few of them have been educated to exercise power.[4]

In our discussions of self-interest in the marketplace we need to assess its impact on the common good from every perspective possible: the effects on investors, consumers, workers, and the environment. We need to ask if present-day profits are worth any substantially negative long-term effects of economic activity.

The classical economists did not ask these questions. Their perception was that the sources of profit (land, raw resources, labor, capital) were unlimited. They did not have any experience of the large corporation, the multinational corporation, or the transnational corporation and their ability to use land, labor, capital, and raw resources in such large quantities. Neither did they experience the automobile and other technologies that enable us

---

4. Silk and Vogel, *Ethics and Profits*, 202.

to wrest raw materials from nature in such gigantic portions. They would probably be shocked at our ability to catch a salmon in the Barents Straits in the morning and serve it on a chafing dish in San Francisco, China, or Australia in the evening.

Their perception was that as businesses grow, more people become employed—a rising tide lifts all boats. They did not see the limitations on resources we see today, and therefore their confidence in the market factors of self-interest and competition were unflagging.

## COMPETITION

The philosopher Wendell Berry writes that if competition is our primary ideal, then we must divide the world up into a class of winners and a class of losers. This kind of division is different from past divisions: ruler and ruled, able and less able, richer and poorer. There is a tension between the past divisions that were tempered by other social and spiritual values, as in the case of the prophets after the time of Moses, who called the king to conversion of heart, to take care of the widow and the orphan.

Competition as the basis of economic systems from a historical perspective is a rather new idea. It proposes to lower cost in any way possible. It needs to be tempered, as other social divisions and philosophies have needed to be tempered in the past, by regulation of raw greed in ways that allow healthy competition.

Adam Smith's time did not witness the cutthroat competition of today's corporations. But it did see the effects the industrial capitalism of its time had on the family. The drive of competition to produce goods at a lower cost than competitors resulted in eighty-four hour, seven-day work weeks, woman and child labor, sweatshop barracks, low wages, and unsafe working conditions. Workers in British and New England factories of the nineteenth century lived in worse conditions and were treated worse than American slaves in the southern United States.

Competition ultimately must be seen in the same way as self-interest: in the light of respect for the rights of all human beings. When competition is nurtured in the context of winners and losers, we need to ask ourselves: What happens to the losers? When massive layoffs occur because of downsizing, few, if any, of the employees who are laid off receive retraining or any other form of compensation. They are merely let go. In the Pacific Northwest of the 1980s, as labor in the lumber mills was cut back and mills were closing by the hundreds, unemployment rose as high as 20 percent in many Oregon communities. No one cared about the losers. They were the sacrificial lambs of outsourcing and selling raw lumber to other countries. When competition is not viewed in the context of rights and duties (i.e., social responsibility), we lose a bit of our humanity.

With the large corporations that exist today, this competition has gone global, in terms of both raw materials and labor. In a later chapter we will discuss the implications this has on labor and the environment, both in wealthy nations such as the United States and in Third World countries such as those in Africa, South and Central America, and Asian.

During the period of the classical economists, there were two plaintive voices that took exception to the majority views of Smith and Ricardo in particular.

One was that of Robert Owen. He ran a successful textile factory in New Lemark, Scotland, in the mid-nineteenth century. His factory ran at a competitive profit, but had the following differences from a normal factory: the employees worked only a ten-hour day and had Sundays off, their families had cooperative housing and gardens which they owned, the salaries were higher, and children did not work in the factory. What Owen achieved at the New Lemark factory is credited with the springing up of consumer and producer cooperatives around Western Europe and the beginnings of the Grand National Union among textile workers.[5]

Another voice crying in the desert of laissez-faire capitalism in the nineteenth century was John Hobson. Hobson warned that the expansionism, which was central to the economic theory of his day, would lead to economic imperialism (economic colonialism) and ultimately war, as nations fought for raw materials. His was not a voice that business interests of the day wanted to hear. So although his insightful evaluation of capitalism's expansionism was valid, his views were not taken seriously by the business community. Such consideration would have demanded change—conversion.

While the classical economists maintained an unwavering belief that the market as self-regulating, and that all boats rise with the tide, the Great Depression that hit the United States in 1929 proved them wrong.

The Depression disproved the tenet of the classical economists that growth of the economy produces jobs and profits, which produces surplus

---

5. Heilbroner, *Worldly Philosophers*, 113.

money in the form of savings and at the same time capital investments of profits in a never-ending expansive cycle.

The Depression proved that an economy can become stagnant, and that there is no necessary connection between the availability of money at a lower interest rate and businesses' willingness to borrow and expand.

The historian William Manchester mentions that in August of 1929,

> a writer for the *Saturday Evening Post* asked John Maynard Keynes, the great British economist, whether there had ever been anything like the Depression before. "Yes," he replied. "It was called the Dark Ages . . . and it lasted Four Hundred Years."[6]

Keynes was an advocate of government intervention in the economy in the form of investment. It was his belief that deliberate spending by government to stimulate the economy would create wages. This in turn would stimulate spending ("priming the pump"), which would then lead to an increase in consumption (buying power), which would lead to business expansion.

The administration of Franklin Delano Roosevelt, to which Keynes served as an advisor, proved Keynes right. Government spending during the Depression and World War II brought full employment in the United States.

William Manchester points out that one of the causes of the Depression was the failure of the level of wages to keep up with the level of production. Industrialization had boosted production efficiency per man-hour by 40 percent, so a lot of inventory (product) glutted a market that people did not have the money (wages) to buy. This was one contributor to the massive business failures. Manchester's point illustrates well the necessary connection between just wages and a healthy economy.[7]

In commenting on Keynes's approach, John Kenneth Galbraith says that in earlier times Keynes, in order to clearly illustrate his theory in a tongue in cheek manner, had proposed that pound notes should be buried in abandoned coal mines—digging them up would add beneficially to employment and purchasing power. After World War II, defense spending became the abandoned coal mine of the United States. We spend billions of dollars on weapons we know we never want to use because they are too destructive. In effect we have been taking Keynes' advice about burying pound notes and applying it to government spending in the area of defense in order to create jobs.

---

6. Manchester, *Glory and the Dream*, 32.
7. Ibid., 33.

## Classical Economic Theory

Whether or not defense is the best area for us to be spending those dollars in terms of creating jobs is a question that needs to be asked. First, is the creation of such destructive force and the accompanying toxic byproducts the best way to spend taxpayer dollars? Second, might there not be other areas of public expenditure that would create more jobs and therefore greater redistribution of wealth than the defense industry?

The time of the recovery from the Depression and World War II through the 1970s witnessed the greatest redistribution of wealth in the history of the United States. Much of this had to do with a combination of a progressive tax code, strong labor unions, and the role the government played in stimulating the economy.

Private enterprise has historically had a negative view of government involvement in business. In the early 1990s, as a developer of affordable housing in the southern Bay Area in California, the company that I headed (a non-profit housing development corporation) was building a site with 114 single-family homes in the city of Milpitas. At the time, federal subsidy programs for low-income home ownership were extremely limited.

We therefore made the business decision to sell 70 of the houses on the site at market prices and use the profits from them to subsidize selling the other 44 of the houses to low-income families.

We applied to the California Housing and Community Development Agency for a loan, which we received. However, during the loan committee meeting, a for-profit residential housing developer on the loan committee said he would be voting against our proposal because he did not think the non-profit sector had a right to compete with the private sector.

I pointed out to him that the private sector of residential developers were competing with me on a regular basis for tax increment funds from redevelopment agencies, federal funds, low-income housing tax credit allocations, even the predevelopment funds for which I was now applying. While he was the only no vote on the committee, I do not think he understood just how often the private sector is at the public trough.

During this same period, a private partnership was building the Fairmont Hotel in San Jose. The cost of the hotel was approximately $100 million. The city of San Jose devoted $33 million of tax increment financing in addition to other tax incentives to make this a viable economic business deal. If one assumes that the profit and overhead of the partnership of the developer would have been in the area of 14–17 percent of the total cost, then taxpayers paid the overhead and profit of the project.

## A Conscious Endeavor

I am not saying it is bad for government (local or federal) to invest in economic growth. But the private sector in this country is the first to want tax breaks and real dollar contributions from the government. At the same time, the private sector criticizes programs such as education, medical care, and welfare, which help people in real need. They are often the first to complain about government regulation after receiving government aid in large sums.

Corporations claim that helping them through lower taxes, bargain government land, mineral rights deals, and oil depletion allowances (i.e., corporate welfare) will make them more productive. However, they also argue that if you give help to poor people in the form of welfare this will make them lazy. One has to question the logic here.

A person to whom conversion is important will want to understand that the private sector in the United States has received more government direct aid (literally in the trillions of dollars) than the poor have ever received. In their book *A People's Charter*, James and Stewart Burns write:

> It was not surprising that the 1877 revolt (general strike) centered on the railroads—the biggest, most powerful, and most unrestrained of the capitalist juggernauts to emerge after the Civil War. Fueled by federal subsidies and by vast land grants amounting to an area larger than Texas, these corporations had laid 80,000 miles of track by 1877 (compared to 2,200 by 1850) and monopolized the transport of people and goods.[8]

It is important to discuss government support of the private sector (I will bring this up again later in our discussion of corporations themselves) because it is so often overlooked, and because questions need to be asked about what public benefit has resulted from this direct subsidy.

For instance, has public subsidy of the private sector had any influence on redistribution of wealth? If your tax dollars are only going to the benefit (i.e., profit) of a very small group of investors or the very top levels of a particular company, is that just? Has public subsidy of the private sector been used to create the highest level of employment possible with those dollars? If not, why not? Has the expenditure of public dollars in the private sector resulted in just wages for workers?

In the corrective measures taken by government intervention during and immediately after the Depression, these were major concerns. They are just as valid now.

8. Burns and Burns, *People's Charter*, 172.

## Classical Economic Theory

When I studied theology years ago, many theologians were criticized as being "ivory tower" academics. This meant they fashioned mental constructs that had no relationship to reality.

Economists of today deserve the same criticism. Milton Friedman is perhaps the one most deserving of it. He seems to think it is possible to consider a world in which competition and self-interest still apply as the only worthwhile considerations in discussing market factors. Even his monetary theory quickly became outmoded as global monetary availability and computers wrested the power of national governments to absolutely control the flow of money through interest rates. One would be hard pressed to name a single corporation or large company since 1850 that did not receive direct government aid in the form of direct subsidy, favorable government leases/purchases, or tax favoritism. The idea that an unregulated economic setting has ever existed is at best a mental construct.

Government involvement has been heavily weighted in favor of private companies and corporations rather than the general citizenry it ostensibly serves. For people like Milton Friedman to make believe that this is not so is the worst form of chicanery. His ideas were formative of the economic agendas of the Reagan/Bush presidencies. His ideas might be considered amusing, except that results of policies formed under his influence have helped create a devastating widening of the gap between rich and poor in this country and in the world in general during the period from 1980 onward. This renewed unleashing of raw greed is not unlike what took place from 1850 until the Depression. One would have hoped we would have learned a lesson.

In 1974 Fletcher Byron, the chairman of the Koppers corporation, said:

> Profits are to a corporation what breathing is to human life. We cannot live without breathing, and a corporation cannot live in a private economic system without profits. But breathing is not the sole purpose of life, and profits are not the sole purpose of the adventure we call business management.[9]

And Frank Abrams, an executive at Chevron, said:

> We like to feel that it is an important place to work. We have equal responsibilities to other groups: stockholders, customers, and the public generally, including government. What is the proper

---

9. Quoted in Silk and Vogel, *Ethics and Profits*, 160.

balance for the claims of the different sections? What part of profits should go to stockholders? What part to the employee's wages? What part to the customer in lower prices and improved quality? Keeping the proper balance in these things is one of the most important matters that corporate management has to consider.[10]

This is quite different from Milton Friedman, who said that "a corporation has only to make profits and keep the rules."

---

10. Quoted in ibid., 134.

# 12
# Life with Corporations

IN THE MID-1980S IN California, MCA was bought out by a Japanese corporation. At the time, MCA owned the concessions, motels, and guest services at Yosemite National Park. There was a great furor about a foreign company having control of concessions in our nation's most popular national park.

The outcry ultimately forced MCA to divest the Yosemite concession (known as the Curry Co.), which was then placed under non-profit management.

There is something inside people of all countries that makes them rankle when any of their perceived national treasures are controlled by foreign interests. It does not seem to matter whether foreign interests control raw materials or foreign control manifests itself in cultural changes caused by foreign interests and foreign investment, such as is occurring in the Middle East. What I am referring to is the "Westernization" of Middle Eastern cultures resulting from foreign investment, and the seeming inability of these cultures to absorb and adapt to this influence in ways that expand and deepen them.

You recall the Old Testament view of our role as stewards of the earth. One of the constructs that human beings have invented for this stewardship is the idea of the country or nation. Nationhood, which is a type of group ownership of a region, is the primary legal agency through which people exercise their stewardship. This is true regarding definitions of legal borders of countries, and the form of government land or economic system under which a country decides to organize its life. It seems that we break down our ownership of the earth first to regions, then territories, and then down to societal ownership and individual ownership.

The scriptural view of things is that all cooperate in this stewardship at every level. No nation, society, or individual has the right to wrest from another nation, society, or individual its ability to be a good steward.

As we try to reconcile the spiritual concept of justice with nationhood and national rights, one of the conclusions we might draw is that the resources of any nation are first and foremost to be controlled and developed in the best common interests of the people of that nation, primarily but not exclusively. Some nations do not have all the resources their people need for a decent life. Such nations might need to secure from other nations the resources they need. They may wish to import these resources and export certain materials or products that they do not need. However, the guiding principle should be that their stewardship should never be sacrificed in such a way that the primary benefit of a business or development exchange goes to some other nation/country beyond what is just.

John Hobson warned us in the nineteenth century that the expansionism inherent in industrial capitalism could lead to economic colonialism, and it did. Economic expansionism exploits labor, capital, or raw resources in favor one nation, group, or interest at the expense of another nation, group, or interest. Our situation today has expanded beyond individual nations' economic interests to include corporations of such great magnitude that their economies are often greater than the economies of many Third World emerging countries/nations. Such corporations have become truly global and transnational. And their ability to take unfair advantage of the labor, capital, and resources of emerging small countries is great, while the ability of even large wealthy governments to control the appetite of these corporations is negligible.

How are we to view what we see happening at the present time with corporations? How does the Judeo-Christian perspective bring a value system that can help us evaluate current global corporate practices?

The Judeo-Christian backdrop will include the notions of respect for the dignity of all people, stewardship, just wages, and just distribution.

As we mentioned in the last chapter, the original thirteen American colonies were established as corporations of the king of England. When the American Revolution occurred, there was no mention of corporations either in the Declaration of Independence or the Constitution. We can conclude that in the early days of the United States that while the founding fathers certainly knew of the legal concept of the corporation, none anticipated the role corporations would come to play one and a half centuries later.

Until the mid-eighteenth century, the United States was mainly a rural economy governed by farms, small businesses, and cooperatives. The real effect of government in the lives of people was local, through states, cities, and towns.

Therefore, in the early life of the United States the power to charter corporations was seen as an affair for individual states. The intent was to keep corporations under local citizen control. Generally speaking, states placed set limits on corporations regarding borrowing, ownership of land, and at times even their profits.

To receive a charter, a corporation had to demonstrate that it would serve a public interest. Charters could be revoked at will if it was concluded the public interest was no longer being served. There have been tensions in the development of democracy alongside the economic system of capitalism in the United States. The concept of democracy in the U.S. developed when the young country had vast raw resources, undeveloped land, and large waves of immigration. Our economic system has developed in a context where there are major differences over the relative emphasis on individual and states' rights, on the one hand, and a strong central (federal) government, on the other. Intelligent men and women can and have come down on opposite sides of this discussion throughout the history of the United States, and this is probably a healthy discussion. In the early days of this country, these opposite sides took the form of the Federalists, which included among others Hamilton and Washington, on the one hand, and the Republicans, which included among others Jefferson and Franklin, on the other. This discussion has at times boiled over into war. The Civil War was basically a war about the rights of states against those of the federal government regarding the economic system in the South, which relied heavily on slavery. The tension and disagreements about the rights of the individual (today's libertarians) against those of the group (those who support government regulation of certain aspects of our common life as a nation) is further complicated by corporations, which, while in reality constitute a group of people, are legally treated as an individual with all the rights of an individual under constitutional law.

Perhaps the tension between individual rights and the common good should remain in open dialogue as each generation of Americans struggles with the concept of democracy. While the discussion is already complicated just considering the rights of individuals as opposed to the rights of the state (a collection of individuals by mutual consent), the legal reality of the corporation further complicates this discussion. On the one hand, we must reflect upon the rights of the individual as they stack up against the common good—a complex question in itself. But in addition we must address what have become the collective rights of economic agencies, which express themselves in the legal reality of corporations. Today, as we have mentioned, this discussion is greatly complicated by the fact that many corporations are truly global and often larger than nations in terms of both their internal economy and their global interest and appetite.

The nineteenth century was a time of great discussion about individual rights and property rights. It was during this time that the feudal tenant farming practices in New York and Maryland were beginning to be revised. Certain families in these states had been given land grants millions of acres each as early settlers. This group had a strong interest in preserving their ownership. Others (one might call them the masses) were demanding small land portions to create farming opportunities. The situation became tense. With a revolution just having been accomplished, the idea of another was something elected officials of the new government did not relish. Stability and demonstrating their ability to govern were seen as paramount. Revolution in New York and Maryland was narrowly avoided by making land reform concessions to the general population. One can site many examples of the conflict between the common good and individual rights in the early life of the fledgling republic.

The first half of the nineteenth century was an age of expansion and definition of national boundaries of this new republic. Some basic solutions to the debate over individual and government rights resulted in the Civil War. The period following the Civil War saw the rise of industrial factories and the Robber Barons (Carnegies, Frick, Rockefellers, Pierpoints, Mellon, J.P. Morgan, Vanderbilt, Philip Armour, and Jay Gould). From the conclusion of the Civil War to the end of the nineteenth century, men such as these were able to literally buy the votes needed to get land grants, bonds, and laws changed that favored their economic interests.

The jewel in the crown of such interests was created in 1886 in the Supreme Court case of Santa Clara County vs. Southern Pacific Railroad. The decision of the Supreme Court that corporations had the rights of individuals became for the average citizen what the Dred Scott decision had been for African Americans. Essentially, the case applied Fourteenth Amendment rights to corporations, allowing them to be considered as "persons." Corporations were given the full rights of individual citizens without necessarily being faced with the same responsibilities. By being guaranteed the same rights of free speech as individual human citizens, corporations were able to attain exactly what the Bill of Rights was intended to prevent: domination of public thought and discourse. The vast amounts of money and power put at the disposal of corporations to influence government mocks the constitutional intent that all citizens have an equal voice in the political debate surrounding important issues.

Prior to WWI there was a great amalgamation of corporate wealth in the U.S. Morgan and Rockefeller joined power to amalgamate 112 corporations under the Northern Securities Corporation. This amalgamation had a value superior to the real estate value of the thirteen Southern states.

During this same period began the development of the labor union movement, which demanded rights for workers (the group) with regard to issues such as wages, health coverage, the length of the work week, and safety conditions, against the power of corporations (individuals) to dominate the discussion of these issues. Again, this discussion often erupted into violent expressions, resulting even in death, particularly in urban industrial areas. The historian William Manchester has written that from the post-WWI era through the Great Depression, if the democratic and economic system of the United States had not defended many of the rights of laborers in this country, there may very well have been a second revolution that would have made the original revolution pale in comparison. There was a time in this country when being a working person meant being poor, and the communist party in the United States was the greatest defender of the interests of labor. Had it not been for the development of a strong labor movement and government intervention in the economy during President Roosevelt's time, the United States as we know it would probably not have survived.

But even with the controls placed on the liberal capitalism of the early twentieth century, macro issues dealing with political influence, global trade, corporate influence over foreign policy, and the role of corporations in the domestic political scene were never curtailed either by the legal system or union efforts.

The outcome has been an ever-expanding role of corporations in controlling the domestic market and influencing foreign policy to assure their competitiveness abroad. This corporate influence has even developed to the point where the interests of many global corporations based in wealthy nations are able to lobby and protect their interests over the interests of the countries in which their offices reside.

In time, corporate business influence took the form of the U.S. government, through the CIA, influencing and sometimes toppling governments that were not friendly to American corporate interests (e.g., the 1954 overthrow of the Guatemalan government to protect the interests of the United Fruit Company, and the 1973 overthrow of the Allende government in Chile to protect IT&T interests). I am not introducing this discussion to bring the reader to the conclusion that corporations are intrinsically bad. I bring this up only to illustrate how difficult and complex the discussion can get concerning the concept of justice and the rights of individuals versus the rights of the group or the wealthy. Where do we draw the line between justice for the common good versus the rights of individuals? How do we control raw greed while encouraging just forms of individual incentive and economic creativity?

Influence peddling has often included the formation of public opinion through the (corporate owned) media. The rank-and-file middle-class, as employees of corporations, have often accepted the philosophy of corporate America without taking a critical look at it: a free market philosophy that dominates practically every strata of American society. In many ways we have accepted at our core the idea that "What is good for General Motors is good for America." The assumptions of this free-market philosophy are materialistic: Ever-expanding economic growth (GNP) is equated with human progress. Economic globalization is beneficial to everyone (i.e., it creates jobs and lowers prices). Privatization is the answer. The government's role is to enforce laws that protect property rights. The government should play no role in regulating corporations. The free market is the best form of government. People vote with their dollars.

By the 1980s, these views had become such a dominating force that the deregulation of the banking industry and the repeal of anti-trust laws governing corporate mergers would usher in a new era of greed that would reach truly global proportions, and would set the stage for the type of free-market competition on a global basis that is allowed under NAFTA (North American Free Trade Agreement) and GATT (General Agreement on Tariffs and Trade). The result has been a concentration of corporate power with minimal accountability to the communities in which corporations work, whether at home or abroad. If one looks at the control, for instance,

## Life with Corporations

of the ADM corporation over agriculture in the world, one can begin to understand what I am discussing this issue.

As corporations have gone global in search of raw materials and cheaper labor, two things have happened. With regard to raw materials, multinational and transnational corporations have been able to successfully influence the politics of the countries where they are getting raw materials. They have supported dictators in developing nations (Africa and South America) who protect their ability to wrest raw materials and labor from these nations. Many corporations have been able to get developing national governments to look the other way regarding certain environmental practices that would not be allowed in the United States. One does not have to travel far to see the results. The maquiladoras in Mexico just across the border from Texas, Arizona, and California have become known for their toxic contamination and the effects this contamination are having on childbirth for women who work in these factories. Nor has the high incidence of industrial accidents in these plants gone unnoticed.

As well, rather than creating jobs in the United States, the outsourcing that has resulted as corporations have set up production in Third World nations has had a destructive effect on labor unions in the United States. Corporations are quite willing to pull up stakes and move to other countries where labor is much cheaper if they believe union workers in the United State are unreasonable. "Unreasonable" usually means an unwillingness to accept cuts in time, benefits, and wages. All of this is in the name of profits.

There are some U.S.-based corporations that maintain a minimal or non-existent production presence in the U.S. They maintain only management, marketing, and financial planning operations in country, but outsource a majority or all of their production (labor). Nike and Goodyear are two companies who employ this approach. The working and safety conditions of the people in these corporations' foreign factories are similar to the dehumanizing levels that existed in U.S. factories in the late nineteenth century.

How is a person to achieve any sense of sanity in such a world? How can we begin in our own conversion process to affect any change that will have some impact? The adage "Think globally, act locally" has special significance.

First, we can begin to educate ourselves about what is going on. There are many resource publications one can read. At the same time, we all need to get in touch with groups that are trying to live more simple, less consumptive lives. Many are beginning to see the appeal of this choice as opposed to the yuppie consumerism of recent years.

## A Conscious Endeavor

Clearly, we need to take a very serious look at corporations. We need to make them accountable at every turn. Just as the Supreme Court's Dred Scott decision was overturned, we might even want to consider overturning the 1886 Supreme Court decision that gave corporations a level of power that was never intended under the Constitution. Should we as a society consider such a repeal, then we would need to re-examine the whole body of corporate laws that has followed.

Such an action could put corporations once again under the strict control of states. This would disallow any level of political contribution by corporations and put to a grinding halt the present lobbying structure of Washington, DC, and state governments.

We could also broaden the accountability requirements of corporations. The original intent of making corporations file tax returns was so that there could be some public oversight of what corporations were doing. We could enlarge corporate disclosure requirements. We could demand (unpaid) public representatives be placed on boards of directors. We could demand stiffer penalties for violations, especially of environmental or job safety laws. We could demand that corporate tax returns be made more publically accessible. We could create stronger protection for employees who report blatant disregard for the common good within their corporation operations.

Perhaps we must look again at anti-trust legislation in the interest of the wider distribution of wealth. We may need to go back to the idea of single-purpose corporations that are strictly regulated by the states. We may need to pass laws that disallow leveraged buyouts and, going even further, prevent corporations from having subsidiary corporations. We may need to outlaw interlocking boards of directors. We may need to initiate a process whereby corporations are reviewed on a regular (four- or five-year) basis to see if they are still living up to their charters. If they are not, states could revoke their charters. Perhaps we need to look at the tax structure of corporations and make sure they are paying their fair share.

Looking at things from a Judeo-Christian perspective, it seems we must do everything we can to re-establish the value of human beings and their inner spirit. A world in which property reigns supreme is destructive of who we are. We are not just about profits, and our being here is not just about power.

Our being here is about stewardship. We must ask questions and hold people accountable for the ways they use the earth. We must examine our own lives in this regard first. Then we will be able to see how it is possible for us to ask others to cooperate with us.

Government, business, and citizenry all have the same sacred trust: to steward the earth in a manner consistent with our nature as human beings capable of seeing and living out Right Relationships. Iris DeMent suggests this when she writes:

> We got CEO's making 220 times the worker's pay,
> But they'll fight like hell against raisin' the minimum wage
> And if you don't like it, Mister,
> They'll ship your job to some Third World country across the sea,
> And it feels like I'm livin' in the Wasteland of the free.[1]

---

1. DeMent, "Wasteland of the Free," *The Way I Should* (Warner Bros., 1996).

# 13

# The National Interest

PERHAPS ONE OF THE least defined and most often used terms in the press and by the White House and Congress is the term "national interest." This is a catchphrase that has sadly come to justify almost any foreign policy or action that defends the economic rights of the United States against some other foreign interest.

Let us take as an example Operation Desert Storm. Concern about the Middle East, particularly Iran, Iraq, Saudi Arabia, and Kuwait, continues to be perceived as being in our national interest. In fact, our involvement in the Israel situation seems really to be only because of our greater concern about oil in that region, and who will control the flow of that oil. If there were no oil in the Middle East, we would probably not have much concern for Israel, which really translates into "stability" in the Middle East.

It is obvious that Desert Storm was a war about oil. It was not about defending a democracy. Kuwait is not a democracy. Kuwait has less equal distribution of wealth than exists in the U.S. Kuwait has de facto slavery. Many Filipino and other foreign domestics are used in whatever fashion their "employers," the wealthy oil barons, see fit.

Saddam Hussein was certainly not a compassionate man. But even he was not the sole reason we became involved. If we could have curbed Hussein's expansionist goals and arranged for him to cooperate with oil-consuming nations to keep the oil price fixed in the manner that has occurred through OPEC, we would not have become involved in a war.

Pure and simple, it was about oil. If one had a son or daughter fighting in that war, it would have been difficult to accept that he/she was fighting to protect the rights of Chevron, Texaco, Exxon, and other large oil corporate giants to make a whopping profit at the gas pump. Corporate wars for profits would have made it even more difficult to accept the death of a son or daughter. It is difficult to "wrap the flag" around that one.

The public relations slogan of that war was "Support our troops!" Not to have been in support of our troops would have been perceived as heartless and lacking in patriotism. Our government knew the real reasons we were there could not be discussed. There would have been marches on the capitol that would have made the 1960s look like a sock hop. The control of the news media by the military during that war was the most guarded and complete in recorded history. We heard only what the government and military wanted us to hear.

Operation Desert Storm is what happens when you have corporations determining foreign policy. Corporate interest (i.e., profits) becomes "national interest." The issues become dollars and cents. Any other discussion is carefully avoided. The *Rocky Mountain News* ran an article by A.M. Rosenthal, a *New York Times* syndicated columnist, in which he wrote:

> With determined concentration, President Clinton has worked a historic change in American foreign policy. Foreign policy amounts to a nation's political, moral and military stance in the world, its role and values. . . . Clinton has made trade the foundation of his foreign policy, far surpassing other traditional American goals and values, like democracy and human rights, and often overriding security interests. . . . Once conservatives could be expected to oppose strengthening communist power. No longer; as the right abandoned anti-communism, the left has abandoned human rights. Once liberals opposed dictatorships that conservatives found congenial. No longer; Democrats grub money from the Indonesian dictatorship and rationalize the Chinese. . . . Also corruptive of democratic values is the liberal/conservative position that the business of the world now is business, so if the right to talk without risk of arrest and torture has any lingering interest, let American business in China handle it.[1]

While this foreign policy approach has gone far from what has been a traditional concern of American foreign policy, the human rights issue will rise again. There has been a time when we realized our lives are about more than profits. Our lives involve other qualitative concerns that are spiritual in nature (justice, compassion, and human rights). Our foreign policy can and ought to reflect these values.

1. Rosenthal, "Clinton Derails Rights for Trade," 83A.

From a Judeo-Christian perspective, the analysis of current concerns (including foreign policy) should begin by looking at our individual lives and conversion processes. Let us say that we became aware that we were not going to able to get Middle Eastern oil and the price of gas was definitely going to go up. The price of food would increase as well, because food delivery would reflect the increase in shipping expenses.

We would then have to look seriously at our particular use of oil and gas. Such an analysis would probably get us to look at a number of issues: cost (our self-interest), effects on the environment of the internal combustion engine, how we might utilize public transportation, and how we might begin to cooperate with others to find modes of transportation that do not use gasoline.

Once having made a personal analysis and discovered ways we might change ourselves, we could then all begin to cooperate with like-minded people to bring about changes in our consumptive habits locally and then throughout world in an attempt to make the market respond. Once we realize that oil really is a limited commodity, we might really push to develop alternative modes of transportation that employ electricity rather than oil-based fuels. We might push to develop light rail in our cities, electric cars, etc.

The process I have just described is the social-change-through-conversion model we have discussed earlier. We can renovate society, as Emerson says, only when we ourselves are renovated.

We need to analyze more carefully each time the term "national interest" is bandied about. We should look critically at the official explanations that serve to justify foreign policy and actions that flow out of such policies. We can then determine if our national actions are indeed in accord with a moral and sane "national interest." "National interest" should be based on what is best for the common good. The public has been convinced by relentless advertising and marketing conveying that the quality of a person's life is most appropriately defined by the amount of one's material possessions and the amount one consumes. Rather than blindly accepting this materialistic philosophy, we need to examine what our real needs are. We might begin to see that we have a greater need in our society for qualities like simplicity, community, compassion, and justice. We might discover that spiritual values are more important to our "quality of life" than owning, possessing, and having.

In chapter 5 we discussed the Old Testament notion that peace within our borders is directly related to establishing justice for the poor. In our own time, uprisings of the poor here (labor unions 1880–1929; WWI veterans' 25,000-man hobo camp in Washington, DC, in 1932; the Civil Rights Movement in the 1960s; the organization of farmworkers' unions) have been means by which the poor have made their plight known.

Our thinking is backward. We seem to engage all our resources to protect ourselves from enemies we perceive to be outside of our borders instead of the enemies within our borders that are destroying us: poverty, ignorance, unjust wages, racism, and destroyed families. This reflection is not new. Charles Dickens has the Ghost of Christmas Future hiding under his robes the children who represent poverty and ignorance. If we follow the advice of the Old Testament prophets, we will do away with the yoke and burden of injustice within our society. We will give our bread to the hungry and provide relief to the oppressed. Then we will have the domestic peace that justice brings.

We must begin to question those aspects of foreign policy that are in place to protect the interests of profits over human rights.

It is also not possible to talk about national interest without mentioning the insane amount of funds the United States and other industrialized nations spend on nuclear armaments, stealth bombers, the Star Wars defense program, and the like.

Americans can get rather emotional when it comes to talking about world stability. The role of the United States military as "peace keepers" since WWII has led to an ever-expanding role. This policing role has resulted in real wars (Korea, Vietnam, Gulf War) and what have been called "police actions" (Granada, Somalia, Haiti, Panama, and Bosnia). We ought to look at these wars and actions in light of the expanding influence of corporations in the formation of foreign policy and the deployment of U.S. troops.

As military actions, some of these have been more successful (Gulf War, Panama, Granada) than others (Korea, Vietnam, Haiti, Bosnia). Because the policies underlying our involvements have been either unclear, or muted, the general populace of the United States has limited itself to evaluating these actions from the simplistic military viewpoint of "Did we win?" or "Did we lose?"

I was born in 1945 and grew up during the Cold War. I remember growing up in an atmosphere of very real fear of the Soviet Union. I remember well the Cuban Missile Crisis. There was a strong feeling we might soon be at war with Russia.

## A Conscious Endeavor

I remember having atomic bomb drills in grade school. I recall the popularity of bomb shelters in the 1950s. The Cold War and the frenetic pace at which we built atomic weapons, long-range bombers, missile systems that could carry ICBMs, and nuclear submarines that had the ability to launch missiles with warheads from under water progressed proportionally to our perception of what we thought Russia was building. And when the Chinese got the bomb, I remember our reaction.

What is strange about this whole recollection is how the mood of the time said the nuclear arms race was quite the rational thing to do. All the nations who had atomic weapons would keep building enough to blow the world up at least one thousand times over. This would serve as a deterrent to war. What could be more sane and rational than having nuclear weapons by the thousands?

Both in looking back and looking to the future, there are a number of points that involve my reflection on the whole "Nuclear Age" reality.

The first is the fallacy of saying the massive build-up of nuclear weapons prevented WWIII. We cannot say this with certainty. To do so would be following the logic of the man from New York who painted his house purple to keep the elephants away. The proof that it worked was that there were no elephants around. The fact that he lived in New York was not taken into consideration.

Of course, the first actual use of atomic weaponry occurred against the Japanese at Hiroshima and Nagasaki on August 6 and 9, 1944. The historian William Manchester provides some interesting reflections on this event in his book *The Glory and the Dream*.

Truman was first briefed on the Manhattan Project on April 24, 1944. At that time he was told that a device would be exploded in Los Alamos in July that would have the explosive effect of one thousand tons of dynamite. Those on the Manhattan Project would later find they had underestimated this effect. The real effect was twenty to thirty thousand tons of dynamite.

> Moral implications were not ignored. The interim committee (whose members included Stimson, General Marshall, James F. Byrnes, Vannevar Bush, Karl T. Compton, and President James Bryant Compton of Harvard) was sensitive to the fact that atomic energy could not be "considered simply in terms of military weapons" but must also be viewed "in terms of a new relationship to the universe." At the same time, the investigators were aware that

every industrialized nation had its community of atomic physicists; nuclear arms were on the way, whatever the United States decided.[2]

When the committee said the bomb could not be considered merely as a military weapon but in terms of a new relationship with the universe, they were right. The force of the bomb was greater than they had imagined. A force had been unleashed that created a light brighter than that of our own sun, and created temperatures in excess of ten times that of the inner core of our sun.

Interestingly, it was not just the bomb, but a combination of the bomb and Japanese reasoning, that ended the war. Even after the dropping of the second bomb on August 9, there was not an immediate surrender. In fact, there was nearly a military coup of the Japanese government by a kamikaze contingent that wanted to continue the war and literally bomb the USS Missouri as it sailed into Tokyo Bay. Had General Anami not been able to talk them out of it, there would have been no surrender, and the war would have continued.[3] Once the bomb had been actually used as a military weapon, the entire industrialized world came to realize its terrible strength.

> Much indelicacy and outright vulgarity of those first days of the Atomic Age can be set down to incomprehension. The concept was too big, it couldn't be grasped all at once.... Sam Goldwyn's unfortunate quip, "That A-Bomb, it's dynamite!" betrayed as much ignorance of nuclear fission as the farmer in Newport, Arkansas, who wrote the non-existent "Atom Bomb Co." at Oak Ridge, "I have some stumps in my field that I should like to blow out. Have you any atomic bombs the right size for the job? ... In savage irony, imprisoned Hermann Goring put it better. "A mighty accomplishment," he said, "I don't want anything to do with it."[4]

The Nuclear Age saw the creation of a force more difficult to contain locally. Before the Nuclear Age, bombs dropped even in such massive amounts as Dresden and Berlin (which killed many more than the Hiroshima and Nagasaki blasts) had only local effect. We were soon to discover things like nuclear winds, and discovered that even bombs dropped on Bikini Island for test purposes might cause radioactive pollution in the atmosphere that might

---

2. Manchester, *Glory and the Dream*, 375.
3. Ibid.
4. Quoted in ibid., 386.

"fall out" over the United States. We would eventually find that the radioactivity caused by the Nuclear Age could end up in our food chain.

The statement by John Kenneth Galbraith that our defense spending has been our way of taking to heart the opinion of John Maynard Keynes that the government should bury one-pound notes in abandoned coal mines to create jobs to stimulate the economy is more true than we would like to admit. The nuclear arms race that followed the creation of that first use of nuclear weapons against Japan has seen a level of spending unseen before in the history of the industrialized nations.

One would think the possession of nuclear weapons would stop all war. One would think that the possibility of such awesome power would serve as the final deterrent to war. However, having nuclear weapons has not stopped any war since it was first dropped: North Korea vs. U.S., Vietnam vs. U.S., Britain vs. Northern Ireland, Iran vs. Iraq, Russia vs. Afghanistan, Bosnia vs. Serbia, Iraq vs. U.N. and U.S., China vs. Tibet, Israel vs. Egypt, Israel vs. Palestinians . . . and the list goes on.

It is true that spending of vast amounts of money on nuclear arms we will never use has become exactly what Galbraith characterized it to be when he compared it to Keynes's encouragement of government spending to stimulate the economy. There are other "coal mines" where the government can bury money to stimulate the economy and to approach full employment. And these other ways to spend federal funds will more greatly strengthen our families and our society than the building of bombs.

Perhaps an even greater hope for us all is that possession of the bomb has not been able to stop movements towards freedom and justice: Martin Luther King in the United States, Marcos out of the Philippines, Duvalier out of Haiti, Somoza out of Nicaragua, Gorbachev in Russia, Apartheid out of South Africa, and the reunification of Germany. Despite the existence of nuclear weapons, men and women who struggle for freedom and justice have not been deterred from doing so.

This gives me hope in our ability to accomplish great things against what seem at times almost insurmountable odds. At the same time, it convinces me that the amount of money we are spending in our defense budget has done and will do no good.

We need to be both humble and careful as we redefine what will be our national interest. At home perhaps we will rededicate ourselves to establishing "liberty and justice for all" within our borders. In our foreign policy we need to assure that what we offer to other countries is accomplished in a manner that allows them to remain in control of their own destiny. We need to have a foreign policy that is economically disinterested in taking products or producing products at the expense of the developing nation, its environment, and its families and cultural life.

This is a more cooperative approach than has been present in our foreign policy for the last sixty years. It is a posture that all the wealthy nations need to incorporate into their foreign policy. On a global level, it will be our cooperation—not our competition—that will bring about world peace.

This is the type of conversion to which we are called on a global level. It is an effort that carries with it great hope and opportunity. As Roy Rogers sings in the song "Hold on Partner":

> So many people and things can get you down, but it only takes one man to turn it around. If you hold on, Partner, good things are comin' to you.[5]

---

5. Rogers, "Hold on Partner," *Roy Rogers Tribute* (BMG, 1991).

# 14

# Profits

IN ANY BUSINESS ENDEAVOR the process that results in the production of goods and services involves many groups. The groups include consumers, workers, raw materials owners, investors, and often, governments.

In the Judeo-Christian tradition the ethics of how all these groups operate as they produce profits is important. In commerce the ethical person is concerned with making sure his/her business decisions result in Right Relationships. In achieving these relationships every individual has basic rights and corresponding duties. This assures that as one secures one's own rights, one will perform one's duty to secure the same rights for others.

We are not meant to secure our own rights at the expense of the dignity and rights of others. As Wordsworth says, "But trailing clouds of glory do we come from God, who is our home." We are meant to acknowledge in our relationships with all other human beings the dignity that each of us shares as a son/daughter of God.

Let us spend some time reflecting on each of the groups involved in business endeavors that we listed above and look at the rights and duties that exist in each sphere.

## A. RAW MATERIAL OWNERS: RIGHTS AND DUTIES

In our scriptural discussions in chapters 5 and 6, we discussed our role as stewards. In chapters 3 and 4 we discussed the whole notion of conversion and how the Judeo-Christian approach to social change, the environment, and really everything is directly related to our own inner change as we try to create Right Relationships in our lives.

We also discussed that part of our role as humans seems to be in being able to discover the essence of things. Obviously we are meant to use the materials of the earth to sustain our lives. Being able to discover the essence of things helps us identify how we can intelligently make use of the resources earth has to offer.

In the chapter on environmentalism (10), we discussed our need to develop a meticulous concern for how we extract and use the resources of the earth.

One of the most basic questions we need to answer for ourselves is one that was raised when we discussed the differences between what economists call cost internalization and cost externalization. Cost externalization is directly related to the question of profits. In our discussion we noted how cost externalization foists some of the cost that results in private profit (gain) upon the community as a whole. This cost externalization often involves an environmental, social, and/or monetary cost to the community as well.

It would be more honest to eliminate cost externalization and instead have the government pay a business directly to subsidize it. Such a form of welfare would not allow the intellectual dishonesty that now pervades the system.

For example, instead of allowing a cattle rancher to graze cattle on government land for free or at reduced cost, the government should compute the value of this grazing relative to the cost of meat in the supermarket, leather in a pair of shoes, and so on. The cattle rancher would be expected to pay this full value, and the government would issue an actual subsidy check to the cattle rancher for that value.

This would make clear a number of things. It would compute the cost externalization factor as a partial cost of the product. It would educate all of us about how much government subsidy it takes to produce affordable meat and shoes. It would bring more humility to political discussions in which rancher Joe Smith becomes involved concerning welfare for the poor, since Rancher Joe is being sent a welfare check as well.

The same could be said for the oil industry, the mining industry, the railroads . . . there is quite a list of corporations and businesses that receive welfare. As I have said before, the point is not to cast aspersions on government (i.e., the people) using tax dollars to assist business or individuals in need. It is to put it all out in the open so that there can be honest discussion concerning these matters.

The other area of cost externalization relates to multinational or transnational corporations using resources (raw materials) from foreign countries. The alternative of not paying a just price for the resource or material should not be considered ethical. This again may necessitate a discussion about the cost of the end product to the consumer. Justice must be our guiding virtue, together with responsible stewardship.

## B. WORKERS: RIGHTS AND DUTIES

In chapter 4 we discussed the New Testament view of worker's responsibility to perform at the highest level for their employer. There is an old expression, "A full day's work for a full day's pay." The two go together. For purposes of this discussion, a "full day's pay" is a just wage. Every employee is bound in duty to work at a level of performance with the honesty, loyalty, and service that corresponds to the virtues of fairness and justice.

Employees should see themselves as critical members of a team involved in stewardship. The goods and services they provide are of importance to the greater community. Their work should be endowed with pride and satisfaction for providing their product and/or service.

The Judeo-Christian tradition has for a long time acknowledged the rights of workers to organize themselves into societies to improve the quality of their lives and work. Our tradition has recognized the right of workers to assure their rights with regard to just wages, working conditions, and other benefits that can appropriately be considered as necessary to their well-being and the well-being of their families. These would include but not be limited to medical coverage, hours of work, certain accommodation with regard to developmental or physical disability, and retirement.

This began with the guilds in the Middle Ages and has continued to the present in the form of labor unions. The Judeo-Christian tradition supports forms of collective bargaining which have as their goal fairness and justice. As we saw in the Scriptures, discussion of wages and other issues was important to the prophets and Jesus. Our discussions regarding the rights of workers to organize for justice should begin by defining the framework of honest and just collective bargaining. This will help us keep the proper focus and let us more clearly point out abuses that might need to be rectified.

It is not possible to discuss the issue of workers' rights without discussing the issue of what is called the "Right to Work." Most simply put, Right to Work means that workers can work in a shop without being required to participate in a union. Obviously there have been tensions between union and non-union workers in Right to Work states. For instance, if Union X goes out on strike, other workers may come in and provide labor in place of the strikers.

Historically, the issue of having Right to Work laws in states and federally has never been one raised by workers. No labor group has ever sponsored Right to Work legislation.

Right to Work legislation has always been and will likely always be sponsored by owners of businesses, be they corporations or individuals. It is often seen as a means to weaken the impact of unions, whose influence they see as a threat. The Judeo-Christian approach would of necessity take issue with any legislation that originated to lessen fairness and justice to workers.

There have been some experiments lately with welfare programs in states. Some states are using their welfare payments to subsidize private business salaries to get people back to work. This approach is certainly a good use of public dollars. It matches public dollars with private dollars to provide people jobs and the opportunity to learn some aspect of a business or trade. An additional question might be asked concerning this experiment: Shouldn't we subsidize welfare recipients to receive a just wage instead of the minimum wage?

## C. INVESTORS: RIGHTS AND DUTIES

There are various forms of investments. These fall into three general categories: direct loans (secured or unsecured), purchase of stock, and limited partnerships. In all three cases investors' liability is limited to the amount of money invested. Either they will make some money, break even, or lose money.

The question always asked is: What is the return on investment going to be? The investor always wants to get the highest return possible. Concern about a healthy return on investment is natural self-interest. The investor needs to ask him/herself the same questions the employer and the employees should be asking: Is the enterprise legal and ethical? Does the enterprise take a responsible and accountable position with regard to environmental issues? Are employees paid a just wage? If the enterprise conducts business in other countries, what is its record with regard to the above issues? Is the return investors are expecting greedy, or a reasonable return relative to risk?

Normally only these questions are asked: What is the risk? What is the return? What is my security? What is my liability? These are certainly valid questions. But if questions regarding corporate responsibility are never asked by those who invest in the enterprise, who will ask them? Are immediate returns more important in the short run than getting answers to these questions?

In the present day, evaluating a company's accountability is typical of what is called the "socially conscious" investor. There are investment groups in the United States that specialize in socially conscious investing. They match up socially responsible companies with socially concerned investors. The questions about risk and return on investment are then asked within the proper context of stewardship. These groups have been able to demonstrate that competitive returns can be the result of a socially responsible perspective.

It is not appropriate in such a discussion as this to point out what rate of return is appropriate, as this is determined to some extent by the market, and to an even greater extent by how responsible the enterprise is. For instance, an enterprise that externalizes costs, does not employ practices that protect the environment, and does not pay just wages will probably pay a higher return than the enterprise that does not engage in these practices and is responsible and accountable.

Until we look as investors at the social costs of enterprises in terms of their effect on the employees and their families, the environment, and ethics, can we claim to be exercising our stewardship properly?

## D. OWNER: RIGHTS AND DUTIES

Owners of enterprises use raw materials, or components that come from raw materials, to provide goods and services. In doing so they employ people, appeal to investors, and may cooperate both with government and other businesses to provide their goods or services. In all cases, what they provide must be perceived in the marketplace as a need.

Business owners have the right to make a profit, assuming that their business is operating in a responsible manner with regard to stewardship, justice, and ethics. You will notice I have not yet used the term "legal." Not all CEOs and/or presidents of industry have a yacht or a summer home, but they all have attorneys. What is legal is not always ethical (see the Supreme Court case Dred Scott vs. Sandford). There are many examples of something being legal but not ethical. The businessperson who is engaged in conversion in the Judeo-Christian tradition is convinced that a moral life is important.

Such an employer will fulfill his/her duty regarding just wages, working conditions, and recognizing talent and rewarding it where appropriate. Such an employer will earn the respect and loyalty of his/her employees.

A problem that has been pointed out by Heilbroner, Galbraith, and Korten is one more endemic to corporations than to small businesses. Up to WWII there was every likelihood the CEO of a corporation was a member of the founding family (e.g., Henry Ford as head of the Ford Motor Company). In the 1920s and 1930s this began to change dramatically, and the management of corporations became a group separate from the owners. The CEO of GMC or Ford or Chrysler will very likely not have the controlling share of stock ownership. His/her board might, but he/she will not. A controlling share of stock ownership may be as little as 20 percent of the stock in some cases.

This means that two things have changed: (1) who the owner is becomes difficult to discern, and (2) while who is in control might be clear, whose interest they represent is often not clear. For instance, when a CEO downsizes a company and from the "savings" (which translates into profits) gives him/herself a three-million-dollar bonus, whose interest is being served?

This separation of management of corporations from ownership of corporations is an important issue, and one that calls for public input. If these issues are raised in the context of the additional concerns we have considered above when we talked about socially conscious investors, I think the answer in each case will be a positive and productive one. It will at least be one that has gone through a reflective process that has considered all possible implications of profit-making activities.

In classical economic theory, there was an assumption that a business must continue to grow and expand. This is not necessarily true. There are many smaller businesses that, by intent, never get beyond a certain size. Many such businesses are healthy enterprises that provide just wages and opportunities for many people. To assume that bigger is better is only an assumption.

It is important that, whether big or small, business enterprises exercise responsible stewardship.

## E. GOVERNMENT: RIGHTS AND DUTIES

Of all the groups mentioned in the dynamic of the business environment, government should have the least amount of rights, and probably the most duties. I should clarify that I am speaking of government as an institution. Government is still best when it governs least. But it does have a proper role of regulation on local, state, and federal levels, but only insofar as it operates with the common good in mind.

It is a common accusation of both liberal and conservative governments that the political party in power responds to their own special interest groups. There is certainly some truth to this.

If some of the actions suggested in chapter 12 with regard to laws regarding corporations were carried out, much of this would be cured. The role of government is to protect our basic human rights. It is to make sure every individual receives his/her rights even when a majority opinion wants to deny the rights of the minority individuals.

With regard to economic activity, the proper role of government in the areas of environmental protection and job and product safety are appropriate. It is also appropriate for government to look closely at full employment issues and what role it can play to insure this. It is also right for government to consider the just wage issue, and the just distribution of wealth.

Assuming that there were laws that disallow the influence of government by corporations, such areas of discussion and possible regulation of corporations could restore a great amount of democracy.

It should be made clear that our government and our economic system are not one and the same, even though there exists a close relationship between them. The public should be able to trust that government will always act in a manner that is in accord with the protection of the rights of the people. As Thoreau wrote:

> Why concern ourselves so much about our beans for seed, and not be concerned at all about a new generation of men? We should really be fed and cheered if when we met a man we were sure to see that some of the qualities which I have named, which we all prize . . . had taken root and grown in him. Here comes such a subtle and ineffable quality, for instance as truth or justice. . . . Our Ambassadors should be instructed to send home seeds such as these, and Congress help to distribute them over the land.[1]

---

1. Thoreau, *Walden*, in *Works of Henry David Thoreau*, 181–82.

# 15

# Community

ROBERT FROST WROTE IN his poem "A Time to Talk":

> When a friend calls to me from the road
> And slows his horse to a meaning walk,
> I don't stand still and look around
> On all the hills I haven't hoed,
> And shout from where I am, "What is it?"
> No, not as there is a time to talk.
> I thrust my hoe in the mellow ground,
> Blade-end up and five feet tall,
> And plod: I go up to the stone wall
> For a friendly visit.[1]

The pace of life Frost suggests in his poem comes out of an experience of what is important. Often in our discussions we have noticed how little time there is for community, enjoyment, relaxation, and appreciation of the people around us.

We proceed at a frenetic pace to acquire as much as we can, only to find, once having achieved a certain level of success, that we are still not happy and are still barely paying the bills. We are then told that if we achieve at the next level then we will be happy. And so a never-ending spiral of "success" is pursued.

Or perhaps we are at the other end of the economic scale. Maybe, like 80 percent of the American workforce, we are only six months away from homelessness. Perhaps much of our time is spent in obsessive worry about how we are going to "make ends meet," and this anxiety again keeps us from

---

1. In Frost, *Poetry of Robert Frost*, 124.

enjoyment and keeps us alienated often even within the context of our own families. We may often ask ourselves "Is this all there is?" as we spend day after day with no nourishment for the soul.

One time when Jesus and his friends were picking and eating some grain in a field on the Sabbath, they were criticized by the Pharisees for breaking ritual Sabbath laws. Jesus replied, "The Sabbath was made for man, not man for the Sabbath" (Mark 2:27).

We have gotten things turned around. We have somehow become convinced that our success is to be determined by how well our business life or commerce is doing and how much money we have. Thoreau reflected:

> After reading Howitt's account of the Australian gold-digging one evening, I had in my mind's eye, all night, the numerous valleys . . . to which men furiously rush to probe their fortunes . . . turned into demons, and regardless of each others' rights, in their thirst for riches. . . . I asked myself why I might not be washing some gold daily. . . . Why I might not sink a shaft down to the gold within me, and work that mine.[2]

We are so concerned with having that the mining of the gold within the human soul goes undiscovered.

Yet there is a yearning in each of us for deeper meaning.

Families need to be liberated from the subsistence level of existence the world of commerce expects them to endure so that husbands and wives, children and parents, have time to enjoy each other.

People also need time to spend with their extended family, be they blood relatives or a circle of friends.

These greater families sustain and enrich us. They overcome the alienation in our lives. As Isaiah would say, they give "strength to our bones" and make us "like a watered garden."[3] Family and community have strong curative powers to nurture a strong society. Everything we do in terms of commerce should be to build such a society. If all life means is work, our fate is a sorry lot indeed.

In her novel *September*, Rosamunde Pilcher has one of the characters, Archie, who lost a leg in Northern Ireland while in the military, say:

> I don't feel bitter and I don't feel angry. Just desperately sad for the people of Northern Ireland, the ordinary decent people who are trying to make a life for themselves, and bring up their children

2. Thoreau, "Life with Principle," in *Works of Henry David Thoreau*, 629–30.
3. Isa 58:11.

> under this terrible, perpetual shadow of blood and fear. And I feel sad for the whole human race, because if such senseless cruelty is accepted as the norm, then I can see no future for us all.[4]

When injustice and senseless cruelty to others and to the earth become accepted as the norm, then our future looks bleak indeed.

I am heartened by men and women who continue to raise the hard questions in their own lives. It is such men and women who keep us from total alienation and self-destruction.

A few years ago I heard an interview on public television with author Ken Kesey. He thought the lack of any experience of community was ripping society apart. Once we lose a sense of community, we no longer feel we are joined to each other. When we don't feel any connection with the lives of others, our life seems to have less and less value. Our own lives can take on a centrality and importance that is not in the proper perspective. When we are part of a community, our individuality adjusts itself to the context of the community and the relationships in which we are involved. When we are alienated from community, our relationship to others is not in proper perspective.

A lack of belonging to community affects how we think, and thus influences how we act. In short, our social morality is affected by our alienation, and can become confused and damaged in such a way as to affect our social relationships. We can end up with a retarded or arrested development of social ethics.

Our age needs to rediscover the value of the human soul (the spirit or inner man/woman) and do whatever we can to nurture it. The experience of community through family, extended family, local neighbor groups, and civic celebrations will help community grow.

Churches could actually provide community if they dropped dogmatic concerns in favor of basic human warmth and acceptance of people.

We must be interested in a just society. When our energies are expended in the direction of the attainment of justice, we will find with time that we will have peace in our borders, as the prophets promised. Our families will be made whole again. Our light will arise in the darkness.

We all need time to talk: talk to our souls, talk to our family and friends, talk to nature, and talk to the God of our own understanding.

---

4. Pilcher, *September*, 321.

# Conclusion

It has been observed that we often become so convinced that past evils will repeat themselves that we make them repeat themselves. Instead of risking a new kind of life, which implies new evils, we would rather keep the old life along with the old evils with which we are familiar. Thus we cling to the evil that has already been ours, and change becomes impossible.[1]

In this discussion, we have said the Judeo-Christian approach to social change and stewardship of the earth begins with changing ourselves—with conversion, not clinging to old evils. As we change and become more loving, better stewards and more just people, like Zacchaeus, all our relationships will change.

Too often we want to change the other person. If only he/she would change. We extend this desire for others to change to our social reasoning as well. If only a certain corporation would stop a particular practice.

We certainly know that we can change ourselves. As we do, our concerns and how we evaluate various relationships, including our relationship to the world's goods, will change. Emerson said:

> A man is like a bit of Labrador spar which has no luster as you turn it in your hand until you come to a particular angle; then it shows deep and beautiful colors. There is no adaption or universal applicability in men, but each has his special talent, and the mastery or successful men consists in adroitly keeping themselves where and when that turn shall be oftenest to be practiced.[2]

Conversion is the process by which we come to show our special talent. Conversion assures that the talent unique to each of us is molded in such a way to always show its most beautiful colors.

1. Merton, *New Seeds of Contemplation*, 106.
2. Emerson, "Experience," in *Essays*, 313.

## Conclusion

When I sat down to initiate this discussion, I was afraid that many readers might take strong exception to its political tone. But the more I have thought about it, this discussion is more spiritual in nature than political. Conversion is a spiritual change in the person. It will have political implications at times. Those who continue to preach a complete divorce between our spiritual perspective and our political perspective exacerbate rather than improve the discussion.

There are times when Jesus would finish a teaching and people would say, "That is a hard teaching!" (see John 6:60). The rich young man did walk away saddened. To give up the root of his spiritual problem, in his case his wealth, was too hard for him.

When we began this discussion, I was not concerned about the politics of the men and women who might read it. Conversion and inner change transcends Republican and Democratic politics, and liberal and conservative philosophies.

Cardinal Joseph Bernardin of Chicago, now deceased, spoke of his impending death from cancer as a great blessing and opportunity.

Death is a constant reminder that we are here for one purpose only: to use the talents we have been given to be the most loving and just men and women that it is possible for us to be.

Politics is not as radical as the Judeo-Christian tradition in getting to the root of things. The most serious problems we have personally and as a society are not really political problems. In that economics, politics, art, and everything we do flows out of our spirit, to that extent the problems in each arena are spiritual in nature.

As an example of what I am talking about here I would like to refer to the obituary written by Mike Glover of the Associated Press on the life of Senator Harold Hughes of Iowa on October 25, 1996. Mr. Glover says of Senator Hughes:

> Harold Hughes, a truck driver who beat alcoholism to become a three-term governor of Iowa and a U.S. senator, died Thursday at 74. . . . Mr. Hughes quit politics at the height of his popularity, retiring from the Senate in 1974 after one term to devote himself to lay religious work and open the Harold Hughes Center for alcoholism treatment. . . . In announcing his departure from the Senate, he said, "Rightly or wrongly, I believe that I can move more

people through a spiritual approach more effectively than I have been able to achieve through the political approach."[3]

The correction of any spiritual problem is conversion, change from within, getting rid of our hearts of stone and getting a heart of flesh instead.

So my concern is not that people will disagree with the politics or economics presented here. I really don't think the discussion encourages resolving issues in only a political or economic way. More than anything, I want to raise questions from a Judeo-Christian perspective. I hope this task has been sufficiently accomplished so that you feel the importance of answering them.

Conversion in the Judeo-Christian tradition means we need to change day by day, bit by bit, to model ourselves after the love of God. Thomas Merton said that no matter how little you may have learned of God in your life, you should compare all your acts to that little bit, so that by and large the habit of love infuses and influences everything you do.[4]

We each need to be more reflective and contemplative in our lives. We need to weigh thoughtfully and morally the implications of our economic and political activities. To allow either to exist in a vacuum is a fatal mistake, as we have seen over the last century and a half.

Don't misunderstand me. I have a very healthy respect for the separation of church and state. I am merely saying, as Emerson said, that a man or woman who is renovated him/herself brings something unique to this discussion of social change. Such men and woman who are involved in a process of self-renovation (conversion) help society to ask the soulful questions and find answers that will nurture the human spirit in all of us.

We have so little literature in our American tradition that deals with dissent and social change. Thoreau is one of the few who gives us much to reflect on. I conclude this discussion with his words:

> I learned this, at least by my experiment; that if one advances confidently in the direction of his dreams, and endeavors to live the life which he has imagined, he will meet with a success unexpected in common hours. He will put some things behind, will pass an invisible boundary; new, universal, and more liberal laws will begin to establish themselves around and within him; or the old laws be expanded, and interpreted in his favor in a more liberal sense, and he will live with the license of a higher order of beings.

3. Glover, "Harold Hughes," 14B.
4. Merton, *New Seeds of Contemplation*, 138.

## Conclusion

In proportion as he simplifies his life, the laws of the universe will appear less complex, and solitude will not be solitude, nor poverty, poverty, nor weakness, weakness. If you have built castles in the air, your work need not be lost; that is where they should be. Now put foundations under them.[5]

---

5. Thoreau, *Walden*, in *Works of Henry David Thoreau*, 356.

# Bibliography

Alinski, Saul. *Rules for Radicals*. New York: Vintage Books, 1969.
Arnold, Matthew. "The Buried Life." In *The Works of Matthew Arnold*, edited by Miriam Allott. Oxford: Oxford University Press, 1995.
Burns, James MacGregor, and Stewart Burns. *A People's Charter: The Pursuit of Rights in America*. New York: Knopf, 1991.
Cannon, Hal. *New Cowboy Poetry: A Contemporary Gathering*. Layton, UT: Peregrine Smith, 1990.
Chesterton, G. K. *What's Wrong with the World*. New York: Dodd, Mead, 1910.
Emerson, Ralph Waldo. *Essays*. Edited by Eugene D. Holmes, revised by H. Y. Moffett. Rev ed. New York: Macmillan, 1930.
Emerson, Ralph Waldo. *The Selected Writings of Ralph Waldo Emerson*. Edited by Brooks Atkinson. New York: Modern Library, 1992.
Fabrikant, Geraldine. "Don't Fence in Ted Turner or His Bison." *Rocky Mountain News*, November 25, 1996, 9B.
Francis of Assisi. *St. Francis of Assisi: Writings and Early Biographies: English Omnibus of Sources for the Life of St. Francis*. Edited by Marion Alphonse Habig. Chicago: Franciscan Herald, 1972.
Frost, Robert. *The Poetry of Robert Frost*. Edited by Edward Connery Lathem. New York: Holt, Rinehart, and Winston, 1979.
Glover, Mike. "Harold Hughes, Ex-Trucker Who Became Iowa Governor, U.S. Senator." *Rocky Mountain News*, October 25, 1996, 14B.
Heilbroner, Robert L. *The Worldly Philosophers: The Lives, Times, and Ideas of the Great Economic Thinkers*. 6th ed. New York: Simon & Schuster, 1986.
Hillerman, Tony. *Sacred Clowns*. San Francisco: Harper, 1993.
John XXIII, Pope. *Peace on Earth [Pacem in terris]: Addressed to All Mankind*. Boston: Daughters of St. Paul, 1963.
Kelton, Elmer. *The Day the Cowboys Quit*. Fort Worth, TX: Texas Christian University Press, 1971.
Kingsolver, Barbara. *Animal Dreams*. New York: Harper, 1990.
Korten David. *When Corporations Rule the World*. West Hartford, CT: Kumarian Press, 1995.
Manchester, William. *The Glory and the Dream: A Narrative History of America, 1932–1972*. New York: Bantam, 1975.
Marius, Richard. *Bound for the Promised Land*. New York: Knopf, 1976.

BIBLIOGRAPHY

Merton, Thomas. *New Seeds of Contemplation*. Gethsemane Monastery: New Directions, 1961.
Mitchell, Stephen. *The Gospel According to Jesus*. New York: Harper, 1991.
Paine, Thomas. *The American Crisis*. Fishkill, NY: printed by Samuel Loudon, 1777.
Pilcher, Rosamunde. *September*. New York: St. Martin's, 1991.
Rinpoche, Sogyal, translator. *The Tibetan Book of Living and Dying*. Edited by Patrick Gaffney and Andrew Harvey. San Francisco: Harper, 1992.
Rosenthal, A. M. "Clinton Derails Rights for Trade." *Rocky Mountain News*, November 29, 1996, 83A.
Silk, Leonard Solomon, and David Vogel. *Ethics and Profits: The Crisis of Confidence in American Business*. New York: Simon & Schuster, 1976.
Thoreau, Henry David. *The Works of Henry David Thoreau*. Edited by Lily Owens. Stamford, CT: Longmeadow, 1981
Tocqueville, Alexis de. *Democracy in America*. Vol. 2. New York: Knopf, 1945.
Whitman, Walt. "The Base of All Metaphysics." In *Leaves of Grass*, 101–2. Garden City, NY: Doubleday, 1926.
Wordsworth, William. "Ode on Intimations of Immortality." In *World Masterpieces*, edited by Maynark Mack, 2: 509–15. New York: Norton, 1956.

www.ingramcontent.com/pod-product-compliance
Lightning Source LLC
Chambersburg PA
CBHW050846160426
43192CB00011B/2164